AVANT-GARDE FILM

FORMS, THEMES AND PASSIONS

MICHAEL O'PRAY

WALLFLOWER

LONDON and NEW YORK

A Wallflower Paperback

First published in Great Britain in 2003 by
Wallflower Press
4th Floor, 26 Shacklewell Lane, London E8 2EZ
www.wallflowerpress.co.uk

A catalogue record for this book is available from the British Library

ISBN 1 903364 56 6

Book Design by Rob Bowden Design

Printed in Great Britain by Antony Rowe Ltd, Chippenham, Wiltshire

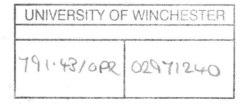

UNIVERSITY COLLEGE
WINCHESTER

Martial Rose Library
Tel: 01962 827306

OTHER TITLES IN THE SHORT CUTS SERIES

CONTENTS

ACKNOWLEDGEMENTS

I would like to thank, as always, A.L. Rees, Simon Field and David Curtis for years of debate, advice, criticism and knowledge. I also owe a debt of gratitude to my colleagues at the University of East London, especially Paul Dave, Mark Nash, Tony Sinden, John Smith, Karen Raney, Russell Hedges, Gillian Elinor and particularly the late Ray Durgnat. Over the years, many other friends, colleagues, students and film-makers have contributed to my views on avant-garde film without necessarily sharing them. Last, but not least, thanks to Sarah for her critical reading of drafts and her patience through it all.

For help in obtaining stills I would like to thank David Curtis at the British Artists' Film and Video Study Collection of the AHRB Centre for Film and Television, Mark Webber and Jayne Parker.

PREFACE

This book is not a definitive account of the avant-garde film. Its guiding idea is to provide a schematic history and at the same time open up some of its themes, forms and motivating passions by way of discussing the films of particular film artists. To this extent it is an introductory book aimed primarily at students and the general reader. Hopefully it will send such a reader to the films discussed as well as to the ones that have found no place in what follows. For a more comprehensive historical and critical exploration of the avant-garde, P. Adams Sitney's classic *Visionary Film* (1979) and A.L. Rees's more recent *A History of Experimental Film and Video* (1999) are both exemplary.

The choice of films has been determined partly by my own enthusiasms and also by the generally agreed importance of some films and film-makers in this tradition. My choice has also been governed to some degree by the availability of films, the bugbear of any teacher and student. I have broken with this condition on a few occasions where excluding a film-maker on such grounds would distort my argument – especially Andy Warhol, Bruce Conner and Jayne Parker. But thankfully, films by Hans Richter, Jack Smith, Stan Brakhage, Kenneth Anger, Maya Deren, Man Ray, Luis Buñuel, Robert Breer, the inter-war British avant-garde and others are now available on video. But many titles are difficult to find even in specialist experimental film distribution archives. Many film-makers and films have not found their way into the book for reasons of space and the book will have achieved much if it encourages the reader to explore this work.

It needs to be said that the book is biased after the 1970s towards British avant-garde film. There are two reasons for this. First, the hegemony of American avant-garde film and in Europe of the formal film came to an end in the late 1970s, and individual countries began to respond more to their own aesthetic tradition and socio-political and cultural situation, especially as the 1980s heralded a period dominated by issues especially around feminism, ethnicity and gender. This splintering along such fault lines led to a more eclectic and hybrid 'avant-garde', encouraged by the academic domination of particular cultural and film theories.

I have also been magpie-like in my use of theories and critical ideas. By and large I have tried to resist them. But where debates exist around work or movements I have helped myself to some of their central concepts in order to shed some light. However, it is well to remember that theories when applied to art are nothing more than models – interpretative systems. The best work is open to many interpretations and not all of them theoretical.

1 THE AVANT-GARDE FILM: DEFINITIONS

There has been little agreement among historians or artists as to what is meant by the term 'avant-garde' in relation to film. Ian Christie justly remarks that it is 'an essentially contested concept, always open to dispute or redefinition' (1998: 453). Like others, I have often avoided the problem of definition by pointing with a Wittgensteinian flourish to the tradition commonly understood by most writers on the subject (O'Pray 1996). This means fudged edges and in some cases exclusions and inclusions (often excluded are Sergei Eisenstein, Jean-Luc Godard, Surrealism, to name a few controversial cases). Of course, it is at these contested fringes that the issue of what the term means is forced upon us, serving at least to remind us that films are rarely made to comply to rigid categories or even social, political or cultural agendas.

A further question is: Why does the term 'avant-garde' survive as a viable term in relation to film and not to other visual arts? There are many answers to this. The most potent may be the simple historical fact that this kind of film-making remains, to this day, marginal to the commercial cinema and art world alike. Unlike painting, where the avant-garde rapidly became the mainstream and where novelty and new forms now seem a necessary part of its institutional framework, cinema remains a popular commercial art with a mass audience. As Gilberto Perez remarks, 'a taste for the movies is still relatively unburdened either by the flattery of belonging to an aristocracy of taste or by the intimidation of not belonging' (1998: 28).

Within this perspective the film-makers who make up the avant-garde are producing films which are fundamentally different to their mainstream counterparts – no-budget, intensely personal and using quite different distribution and exhibition circuits. Murray Smith sums it up well:

> The avant-garde is an 'artisanal' or 'personal' mode. Avant-garde films tend to be made by individuals or very small groups of collaborators, financed either by the film-makers alone or in combination with private patronage and grants from arts institutions. Such films are usually distributed through film co-operatives, and exhibited by film societies, museums, and universities. (1998: 395)

Importantly, they also form a quite separate tradition of their own, one which this book addresses.

The notion of the 'avant-garde' also raises the controversial question of value. A classic account was that of the art critic Clement Greenberg (1992) who divided the art world into the avant-garde and the *kitsch*, which included Hollywood films, and where aesthetic value attached to the former. The film avant-garde is renowned for its opposition to mainstream cinema, whose artistic value it has denied and has assigned to the kitsch – the sentimental, melodramatic and banal. This critique is often couched in terms of the mainstream film-maker's meagre artistic control and consequent subservience to the conventions and banalities of ideology demanded by a mass audience. But historically this antagonism is not so clear cut. Not all avant-garde film-makers have eschewed the commercial field. On the contrary, they have often relied on it for financial reasons and even for the creative opportunities it offered. For example, the early abstract animator Oskar Fischinger made advertising films in the 1920s and was involved, albeit briefly, in Disney's kitsch masterpiece *Fantasia* (1941).

But avant-garde film-makers like Jack Smith and Jeff Keen have celebrated aspects of the mainstream Hollywood cinema, especially its tackier 'kitsch' end. Avant-garde film-makers have also embraced – or at least been sympathetic to – what is called 'art cinema', which has combined artistic ambition with commercialism. The arch-avant-garde American film-maker Stan Brakhage has written sympathetically about Carl Theodor Dreyer, D. W. Griffiths and F. W. Murnau, and the famous Anthology Archive set up by avant-gardists included the same film-makers and more in its canon (Brakhage 1977; Sitney 1975). It is an awkward fact that all of these types of cinema – mainstream, art cinema and the avant-garde – lay claim to art. But these types of cinema are primarily categories of practice and not necessarily divided by different categories of what accounts for *art*.

I would like to make a very general distinction between film-makers who have borrowed an avant-garde attitude, subject-matter or desire from the more established visual (at times literary) avant-gardes of painting and sculpture, and those who have pitched their tents within the film tradition itself. The former (e.g. Hans Richter, Walter Ruttman, Malcolm Le Grice) quite obviously have a clarity of ambition and of visual look not shared by the latter (e.g. Maya Deren, Kenneth Anger). It also suggests quite different moments of avant-gardism – for Richter *et al.* the notion of the avant-garde is one shared with well-established art forms like painting, music and poetry. For Anger and others it is one earned against the steady momentous flow of mainstream cinema. This is simply to acknowledge the fact that cinema by and large escaped modernism (but not modernity) in the twentieth century and yet, in the name of entertainment, produced artists – Alfred Hitchcock, John Ford, Fritz Lang and Jean Renoir, to name but a few.

If we do acknowledge an avant-garde then we need to consider what it is the avant-garde of. In art history the term 'avant-garde' was originally used to describe French painting of the early decades of the nineteenth century (Nochlin 1967). It represented an aesthetically and politically motivated attack on traditional art and its values. Borrowed from socialist politics in the same period, 'avant-garde' is a military term denoting an advanced group forging an assault on the enemy ahead of the main army. With film in mind, we may ask who represents the main army and who the enemy? The main army could be the 'true' idea of cinema and film itself and the enemy, the dominant traditional cinema. Or the main army could be mainstream cinema, and the avant-garde its advanced group foraging for new techniques, forms of expression and subject-matter.

However, the term 'avant-garde' is commonly encountered in the context of twentieth-century modernism. It describes modernism's founding
moments in art movements like futurism, dada and cubism. This has led
to the two terms – avant-garde and modernism – being treated as syn-
onymous. But, as Paul Willemen argues, the avant-garde implies a set of
historical relations ... in contrast, the notion of modernism reduces artistic
practice to a set of formal procedures (1994: 143).

For Willemen, modernism is more like a period style, such as cubism or
impressionism, while an avant-garde denotes a historical moment of specific activities and practices not necessarily associated with any particular
artistic style or strategy. Raymond Williams accepts the difficulty of easily
distinguishing modernism from the avant-garde, but suggests:

> Modernism has proposed a new kind of art for a new kind of social
> and perceptual world. The avant-garde, aggressive from the begin-
> ning, saw itself as a breakthrough to the future: its members were ...
> the militants of a creativity which would revive and liberate human-
> ity. (1989: 51)

While modernism dominates the twentieth-century art world, there are a
finite number of avant-gardes and not all of them are necessarily espous-
ing the cause of modernism – surrealism is a case in point.

Andreas Huyssen claims that the avant-garde is primarily a historical
term denoting a particular short-lived period whose radicalism cannot
be repeated thanks to the repressive tolerance of 'Western mass mediated culture in all its manifestations from Hollywood film, television,
advertising, industrial design, and architecture to the aesthetization of
technology and commodity aesthetics' (1986: 15). This introduces the
distinction between the notion of the 'avant-garde' used as referring to a
particular *historical* moment and one denoting a *kind* of activity or practice.
For Huyssen, any potential genuine avant-garde, as opposed to the *neo-*
avant-gardes encountered in contemporary art, would more likely occur
in non-art practices outside the 'culture industry'. But Huyssen does not
address the unique conditions of so called 'avant-garde' film, in fact he

does not refer to it at all, even managing to discuss Andy Warhol without mentioning his film work.

Historians and critics of the film avant-garde have themselves been extremely wary of the term. Of the classic accounts of such film-making, only P. Adams Sitney (1979) has embraced the notion, even if identifying it with what he calls 'visionary film'. Scott MacDonald has also opted for the term 'avant-garde' arguing that it has the 'widest currency' and 'is generally understood to refer to an ongoing history that has been articulated in different ways in different places' (1993: 16). For Laura Mulvey (1996), the film avant-garde is to be understood at times as being the 'negation' of dominant cinema. David Curtis, A.L. Rees and others settled for 'experimental' (Curtis 1971; Rees 1999), a term that was also popular in Britain in the 1940s (see Manvell 1949). Yet the problem with identifying avant-garde as experimental film is that experiment proliferated as we might expect under the conditions of the new medium, for example *The Big Swallow* (Williamson's Kinematograph Co., c.1901). Experiment is marked in commercial mainstream film-making too. In fact, Eisenstein admitted to the innovations of Griffiths for his own film ideas. Equally, experiment tends to denote changes in technique, in methodology; it does not herald an avant-gardism but simply provides traditional cinema with more variety of expression. The experimental tag also suggests tentativeness and quasi-scientific rationalist motivation. It fails to capture, and in fact seems to exclude, the passions and spontaneity involved in many of the films it purports to cover. Similarly, experiment does not imply radical social or political ideas often associated with the avant-gardes. In fact, experimental techniques are to be found in the conservative film tradition used for equally conservative ends.

Furthermore, Sheldon Renan and Parker Tyler both used the term 'underground' (Renan 1967; Tyler 1974); David E. James, in his political contextualisation of the postwar American film avant-garde settled for the distinction between a political and an aesthetic film avant-garde (James 1989); while Malcolm Le Grice opted for 'formal' and Peter Gidal has used 'structural-materialist' and latterly 'materialist' (Le Grice 1976; Gidal 1977, 1989). For Maya Deren, Jonas Mekas and others, the expression 'poetic film' was used to distinguish a tradition stretching back to the 1920s (see Wolf 1997). Each of these terms denotes a nuance, a certain difference of approach, and at times acts as a means of excluding (or including) particular films. For example, 'underground film' is usually identified with the influential American 'beat generation' of the 1950s. But it was originally used, paradoxically, by the film critic Manny Farber (1971) to describe contemporary Hollywood 'B' movies.

'Underground' has also been associated with a social, sexual and cultural sub-culture operating 'beneath' the traditional mainstream. Its metaphorical import is quite different to that of 'avant-garde'. It does not suggest attack but evasion. Unlike the inter-war European avant-garde it never seriously countenanced revolution and seemed happy to carve out its own individualist bohemian niche in American culture, even when it meant a conflictual relationship with it. It had no Marxist reference points, but rather a Romanticist exploration of sexuality, drugs and consciousness-raising. It was the politicisation of European film-makers in the early 1970s which re-introduced the notion of avant-garde displacing the commonplace 'underground'.[1]

Finally, the avant-garde has been traditonally understood as a reaction to realism (Burger 1984; Greenberg 1992). But there are problems in this opposition, for it can be argued that film is intrinsically 'realist' in its mechanical photographic reproduction of reality (as hold André Bazin, Stanley Cavell, Gilberto Perez). In fact, the outburst of non-live-action abstract animation in the German avant-garde of the 1920s marks one of the few film movements to break almost totally with realism. But there are general problems in the association of anti-realism with avant-garde modernism, especially if we treat the realist aspects of Manet and Courbet's paintings as founding artefacts of 'modernism' (see Rosen & Zerner 1984). Equally the abstraction aesthetics of paintings in the early years of the twentieth century had a sense of the real in the ancient Platonic sense of there being a basic 'reality' of forms beyond the surface impressions of ordinary perceptions of the world. In other words, geometric shapes and colours themselves embodied a 'reality' in its most fundamental sense.

In recent years, the contemporary art gallery has embraced film and video, after neglecting them for decades. As such, avant-garde film (and video) has finally joined the other visual arts in an art mainstream demarcated by respectable critical and academic discourse. Their inclusion in the art museum with all that that entails in terms of film's commodification and cultural acceptability signals the end of its 'avant-garde' marginality. But it does not necessarily signal the end of films dedicated to contesting and overthrowing such 'commodification' or 'cultural acceptability' – that is, an avant-garde.

In the end, all of these nomenclatures – avant-garde, underground, experimental, modernist, independent – share some sense of outsideness, of marginality, of independence. And perhaps that is all that can be gleaned from these different formulations in a short introductory book. But this lack of definition is also a measure of the film avant-garde's restlessness. This book does not attempt to resolve the problem. That remains a quest for future researchers.

1   It is often forgotten that in the early years of the British avant-garde, famous for its conceptual rigour, the word 'underground' was rife (see O'Pray 1996; Le Grice 2002).

2   THE 1920s: THE EUROPEAN AVANT-GARDES

The film avant-gardes that emerged in the 1920s remain a potent influence to this day. They form part of probably the most creative period of twentieth-century avant-garde activity across the arts and are the indisputable models of avant-gardism. Indeed, the culture of the entire period was avant-garde.

The 1920s is a complex decade, one of myriad interrelated art movements, fashions and artists, still being unravelled by historians. Such art movements as Dada, Surrealism, Constructivism, Expressionism, de Stijl and others co-existed at the same time, with some artists like Hans Richter flitting from camp to camp (Rees 1979). The idea of the avant-garde, carried over from its first use in French painting of the early nineteenth century, is thus tossed around, argued over, and both rejected and embraced throughout the 1920s and into the 1930s.

The 1920s avant-gardes are also characterised by the cross-fertilisation of art forms – ballet, painting, poetry, music, sculpture, fashion, literature. These high-art sources are matched by an avant-garde fascination with and love of the popular 'low-arts' of circus, vaudeville, Hollywood silent comedies and puppetry. Thus in many ways, the avant-gardes saw their role as being both in opposition to high art and attempting to displace it, to become a new 'high art' so to speak. The precursor of such activity was the pre-World War One Italian Futurist movement which was anti-bourgeois, celebratory of modern urban life and culture, and interestingly included film in its multi-media practices (see Corra 1973; Tisdall & Bozzolla 1977).

Many of the early 1920s avant-garde films are now canonical – Man Ray's *Return to Reason* (1923), Fernand Leger and Dudley Murphy's *Ballet mecanique* (1924), René Clair's *Entr'acte* (1924), Marcel Duchamp's *Anemic cinema* (1926) and so on. Spread over many European countries, but centred mainly in Germany, France and the Soviet Union, with minor outbursts in England, Belgium, Poland, Czechoslovakia and the USA, the 1920s avant-garde established many of the genres and forms that shaped the subsequent film avant-gardes. Abstraction, collage/montage, anti-narrative, poetic, text and image, were all first intimated – even explored – in this period.

The 1920s film avant-garde in Western Europe is dominated in Germany by the graphic animation films of Hans Richter, Walter Ruttmann, Oskar Fischinger and Viking Eggeling (a Swede), who were inspired and motivated by painting, graphics, music and the period's general air of experimentation. Running parallel to this activity was a French avant-garde rooted in the hot-house of Dada and Surrealism. Leger, Duchamp, Man Ray and the surrealists Luis Buñuel, Salvador Dali and Germaine Dulac were its leading artists. In the Soviet cinema two figures dominated – Sergei Eisenstein and Dziga Vertov – who will be discussed in the next chapter.

The 'first' French avant-garde

In many historical accounts of the avant-garde film, the contribution of the early French or 'impressionist' avant-garde is often neglected. One reason for this is its overshadowing by the 'other', extremely influential, art-based avant-garde discussed above. Furthermore this earlier French avant-garde, associated with Jean Epstein, Louis Delluc, Germaine Dulac and Abel Gance, was an experimentally-tinged narrative art-cinema embedded in the commercial sector. Between the end of World War One and the late 1920s, it also produced a large and varied amount of fascinating writing on film, including the avant-garde, most of which remained untranslated until the late 1980s (see Dulac and Epstein in Abel 1988). This early avant-garde was also responsible for the emergence of a supporting network of cine-clubs, film journals, critics and specialised cinemas, thus establishing an infrastructure which became a model for all future avant-garde film practices (see Abel 1988: 281).

The French 'Impressionist' avant-garde was inspired by the desire to make film an art form, and to that end it explored the idea of a 'pure cinema'. It is well to remember that a result of World War One was the lasting ascendancy of the American film industry over the French. The 'Impressionist' idea of making film a specific medium with its own autonomous essence as art demanded distancing their own films from the mainstream popular cinema, although the French avant-garde sought a popular audience itself. The claim for film as the sixth art was already underway in the pre-war period in France.

Another reason for the early French avant-garde's relatively low profile is its fundamentally 'poetic' approach to cinema, often dealing with reverie, visions and dream-like states, as in Jean Epstein's *La Chute de la maison Usher* (1928), Germaine Dulac's *Coquille et le clergyman* (1927), or the Russian emigre Dimitri Kirsanoff's *Menilmontant* (1924). However, in Abel Gance's work (*La Roue* [1922–23], for example), there is the more fashionable, hard-edged machine-aesthetic. Compared with the German experiments, the 'Impressionists' seemed to owe more to late nineteenth-century symbolism and impressionism than to full-blooded modernism. But this can be misleading as Epstein, Gance and others were very much influenced by early modernism and can be seen to be the first group of film-makers to explore the film as a means of representation and not simply as a medium of storytelling (see Abel 1988: 290-4).

The influential theoretical idea of the period was Epstein's notion of 'photogenie', by which he attempted to explore the idea of the camera as a revelatory instrument of reality itself – a precursor of André Bazin's ideas on film realism. Thus, unlike the 'montage' view of film as a series of interconnected shots, the French avant-garde underlined the relationship between the camera and reality. However, editing had its place. Epstein used insert shots of the water's surface as images of states of mind in his version of Edgar Allan Poe's *The Fall of the House of Usher*. This symbolist aesthetic, where the image expresses a feeling, flows from nineteenth-century French poetry (Verlaine, Rimbaud, Mallarme, Baudelaire *et al.*) into modernism through Ezra Pound's 'imagiste' poetry and T. S. Eliot's early poems and, closer to home, Maya Deren's films.

Film techniques – soft-focus, dissolves, close-ups, slow-motion, image distortion – were identified by some of the French avant-garde as central and conducive to artistic expression (Dulac 1987: 305–14). Epstein was careful to make his claims for film art more general realising that a stress on such techniques led to fashion which he saw as the end of a style (Epstein 1978: 26). For Epstein, 'photogenie' was a fairly obscure notion which rested on the idea of the camera capturing 'personality' in film, where that referred to objects, persons and events. At times it could mean a form of impressionism, imitating the detailed focus on reality of French painting which verged often, as in Monet's paintings, on abstraction, or on a rather 'distorted' view of the world, as in Seurat's pointillism.

While this early avant-garde was decidedly against academicism in art it was definitely not as anti-art as Dada and, to some extent, Surrealism proclaimed themselves to be. It did not have strong social or political objectives as did Surrealism or Soviet cinema. Its avant-gardism was largely understood in the nineteenth-century sense of the term, as being at the cutting edge of its medium: it was advancing the art of the cinema. The problem was that there were countless views of what that 'art' should be.

Abstraction and the German avant-garde film

The second decade of the twentieth century witnessed the burgeoning of abstract painting by such influential artists as Malevich, Arp, Kupka, Kandinsky and Mondrian. Munich was one of the European centres of this activity from which emerged the German film avant-garde. Known as the *graphic cinema*, and the *absolute cinema*, the German-based artists who comprised it were never a coherent group but a rather loosely associated one, with a particularly strong relationship existing between Richter and Eggeling.

Abstraction in film was not the hard-won battle witnessed in painting some years earlier. In fact film benefited enormously from the end result of the 1910s, adapting abstract painting's formal ideas by inventive filmic devices. It was not the first attempt at film abstraction. The futurists Ginna and Corra had handpainted film as early as 1910. But it was the first concerted engagement by a group of film-makers with modernist ideas of abstraction culled from painting and, importantly, music (see Vergo 1980). The four film-makers – Richter, Eggeling, Ruttman and Fischinger – worked in the interstices of early abstraction and the iconoclasm of Dada.

Two views of abstraction can be seen to operate at this juncture. First there is a fairly purist Platonist notion in which the essence of reality was taken to be abstract geometric forms like circles, cubes, cylinders, spheres et cetera. In this type of film the result is the representation of a representation – the basic state of animation. This vied with the rather different idea of revealing the abstract or forms existent in reality – a form of abstractionism. In this way a constructivist aesthetics mingled with a Dadaist upturning of normal perceptions and prejudices (see Haas 1984). Charles Harrison has made the distinction between a weak and strong sense of abstraction, where the former still resembles something, although exactly what that something is may be difficult to discern – for example Picasso and Kandinsky. The strong sense is a picture that has no reference to any thing, person or event. Cubism can be seen as abstract in the weak sense while Mondrian's paintings are archetypically strong abstraction.

Abstraction also raises the crucial matter of meaning. For example, in Marcel Fabre's proto-futurist film *Amor pedestre* (1914) its ostensive sub-ject-matter – the feet of a couple – would seem to derive its primary mean-ing from our recognition of what the image contains. The overall secondary meaning may be about the infidelities and hypocrisy of the bourgeoisie. Its filmic form of never showing the protagonists' bodies would also com-plicate the expressive meaning of the film and so forth. In contrast, it may be argued that the meaning of an abstract film is concerned purely with formal relationships – shape, size, depth, movement or colour (some of the films were tinted).

But this purely formal approach to meaning in abstraction is simplistic. While Richter's early films, for example, suggest a purely formal meaning, this is not the case in Walter Ruttmann's work, where there is a definite expressiveness in his manipulation of the formal elements of shape, movement and so on. His films have a sensuousness, a dramatic rhythm and a quality that can evoke feelings akin to those experienced when listening to music – of calm, of agitation and so on. There is an expressive meaning, albeit less precise perhaps than that in the futurist film. This ties in with the centrality of 'irrationalism' in early modernism when understood as 'the liberation of subconscious processes, and the transformation of human consciousness' (Butler 1994: 263). Christopher Butler has argued that Dada stratagems, for instance, are to be seen not simply as contextual and historical aspects but also as subjective, psychological responses by artists in which their own authenticity and expressive needs are crucially at stake.

Hans Richter: Rhythmus 21

Richter's *Rhythmus 21* (1921) uses techniques by which the filmic illusion of space and especially depth is creatively explored. It uses only squares and rectangles, unlike the work of Ruttmann, who was to use continually transforming rounded, curving shapes suggesting organic, and at times, anthropomorphic forms. Malcolm Le Grice describes Richter's films as embodying the 'physical rhythms of movements in space' (1976: 26).

Rhythmus 21 opens with the black screen being squeezed between two white rectangles moving towards each other from both sides of the screen. Equally, in gestalt fashion, it can be seen as a black screen moving inwards through a succession of narrow rectangles to reveal a surrounding white space on either side. The effect is one of movement on the plane of the flat screen. The next shot is of a black square receding into a white space – which is repeated and then returns to the same movement as the opening sequence except the movement is between the top and bottom of the screen. The rest of the film is comprised largely of squares and rectangles moving back and forth into screen space. At times three to five squares and rectangles are moving (sometimes overlapping) at different rates and times to create a complex movement of visual counterpoint. Originally the shapes were coloured (tinted) but most available prints are black and white, leaving only various tones of grey to suggest the original colours (see Moritz 1997).

Rhythmus 21 can be divided into two parts – dark forms in a white 'space' or on a white 'surface' which precedes the reverse strategy. However, it does represent a particular aspect of abstract film (Moritz 1997; Rees 1999). It is also a film that tests our linguistic capacity for describing it. Our choice of words commits us to an ontology of the film – that is, what kinds of things does it comprise? Put more bluntly, how do we describe what we see? Are we dealing with a surface or a space for instance? This is a problem endemic to abstract painting. While these films are sometimes placed in what is called the anti-illusory tradition, they deal fundamentally with perceptual illusions. For example, filming a gradually smaller cut-out square gives the impression or illusion, when projected, of a single-size square receding rapidly into space. To perceive it simply becoming smaller on a flat surface (how it was produced in fact) takes much perceptual effort.

For Richter, these films of the early 1920s were not about form but movement. According to this view, the forms were not discernible as they were only articulated in movement itself. What one perceived was the relationship between positions of a moving shape. Thus, for Richter, what you see in his films is 'a kind of rhythm'. Much of what counts as avant-garde here rests on a thorough-going experimentalism in relation to how film can manipulate perception. Much of its results are related to our normal optical responses and prejudices.

If we compare Richter's film with Eggeling's *Diagonal Symphony*, we can see for the first time a clarity and precision in the latter film's use of abstract forms. But these are not the basic geometric forms of the Platonist tradition – squares, circles, spheres, cones, cubes – but rather quite studied complex shapes falling between abstraction and some kind of symbolic notation system akin to crotchets and quavers in music. It is a more thoughtful and complex metaphysical form of abstraction, more resonant, as its title suggests, with ideas related to music in its fuller sense.

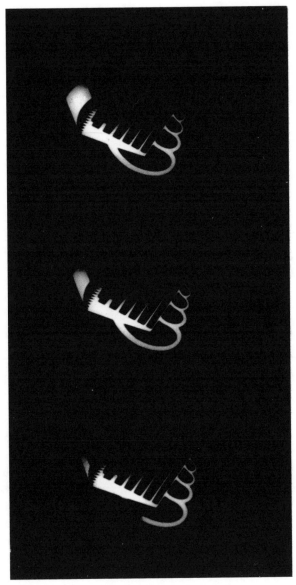

Figure 1 *Diagonal Symphony* (Viking Eggeling, 1922)

In other words, it has a complexity akin to musical forms. To this extent, it has a strong and more genuine sense of a language being developed in terms of moving shapes. It is intensely frame-based and not aligned with the early experiments founded on conjoining shots, which also claimed to be evolving a film 'language'. It is also worth remembering that Eggeling was involved in the Dada movement and his strange patterns and shapes are just that – irrational expressions of a subjectvity that cannot be safely assigned to some philosophically-based abstract system.

Unlike Richter's basic geometrical shapes, Eggeling's are complex imaginative abstractions reminiscent of both hieroglyphics and at times, mundane objects like combs and jugs, as if they were 'symbolic traces' of existent objects, as Charles Harrison has described Kandinsky's paintings (1993: 214). But Eggeling lacks Kandinsky's compositional overallness. His animated shapes instead stand alone, isolated in the film frame suggesting flatness and sometimes depth as the precise figures grow in size, permitting a purely perceptual sense of them coming out of a deeper undefined space.

Crucially, Eggeling uses subtraction and addition in relation to a recurring family of shapes on a flat surface. Where the metamorphisis of forms occurs, it is not through techniques accentuating the free running line or transformation of shapes through illusory manipulations of depth and space, but through flat forms akin to abstract drawings or decorative 'symbols' found on romanesque churches. It is a fairly dry metamorphosis of subtraction and addition as mentioned and not organic as is Fischinger's work. Equally, lack of spatial references or size scale allows imaginative scope for the viewer. In short, any tendency to *anthropomorphise* is radically closed off.

Eggeling's use of the diagonal is interesting for its obvious expressivity again compared with Richter's fairly squared-on films and Ruttmann's fluidity across the screen. Eggeling's diagonals concern not only the shapes which seem to be set at a diagonal angle although that is illusionistic as there is no reason why they should not be such sloping shapes in the first instance; they also lie less ambiguously when there is more than one figure composed diagonally across the screen. This creates a line of compositional force by pulling and pushing against the screen's rectangularity.

There is no real sense of off-screenness in the film, unlike its imaginative use in Ruttmann's work.

Walther Ruttmann: Lichtspiel Opus 1

In *Lichtspiel Opus 1* (1921) Ruttmann presents a quite different sensibility to Richter's or Eggeling's. It is at once more sophisticated in technique and creative expression, with a sensual and, at times, almost erotic pulsation as curved forms voluptuously balloon in and out of the frame. No longer is there the strong feeling of experimentation but instead a fully developed aesthetic of urgent expressive power; William Moritz comments on the film's 'vivid, cogent, dynamic and rhythmic' qualities (1997: 222). The film was originally tinted and made for musical accompaniment by the composer Max Bunting to be performed in public in 1921 but rarely after that, perhaps due to the problems encountered in organising a live, rehearsed string quintet for screenings. It has only recently been reconstructed as it was intended.

Shading and colour also give solidity and volume to *Opus 1*'s shapes, establishing a kinship with drawing as against the more flattened optical experimentation of Richter. Ruttmann's efforts form a parallel with the American cartoonists' black-and-white graphic efforts in the 1920s. For example, in Max Fleischer's Felix the Cat series and Disney's early Mickey Mouse cartoons, the respective animal's black circular shapes were persistently forced to their representational limits by the creative desire to manipulate shapes for their own sake – an impulse that led to Disney's ambitious 'art cartoon' *Fantasia*.

Ruttmann's swooping full-bodied circular shapes, like huge teardrops, florid-edged art deco waves, or continually changing basic biological cellular forms, represent one of the highest achievements of avant-garde film.

Abstracting reality and the French avant-garde film

Dada and abstract art developed in tandem during the 1910s and early 1920s. Dada negated the past bourgeois world while abstraction began

17

to build a utopian future around a new visual language. They were often united in their attitudes to contemporary values both in art and in the world. The Dada artists of the early 1920s became the surrealists of the mid-1920s. Man Ray's films can be seen as transitional between the two movements. What is remarkable about the period is how many of the films produced are difficult to categorise – are they abstract, dadaist, surrealist or some heady mix of some or all? Claims and counterclaims by the film-makers themselves and contemporary observers and collaborators do not help (see Elsaesser 1987).

Man Ray: Return to Reason

Return to Reason (1923) is a fine example of this Dada-Abstractionist tendency. Commisssioned by Tristan Tzara in 1923 for the soirée *le Coeur à Barbe*, it uses for the first time on film Ray's photogram technique developed in 1921. Although primarily seen as a Dada film, *Return to Reason* does however play with formal/abstract patterns in a way that renders murky the distinction between *abstraction/constructivist* ideas and those of Dada. In its images of ordinary objects, its use of text, its scenes mingling with those of the female nude, *Return to Reason* exemplifies the bricolage tendency of Dada while at the same time foregrounding film not simply as a *recording medium* but as a *material system*. By placing tacks and nails and iron filings on the film strip itself, Man Ray furthered the idea of the camera-less film and asserted film's photographic qualities derived from the darkroom, creating a concatenation of black and white shapes *abstracted* from their naturalist-rendering by the traditional cinema. In this way, its spontaneity and refusal of structure is subtlety grounded by an enthusiasm for shape, form, texture, light and movement. The film thus exemplifies the abstracting from reality aesthetic, as Le Grice comments about the film: 'close-up shots of a torso and paper rolls are filmed in such a way as to maintain an ambiguity about their object nature and identity' (1977: 34).

The film begins with a moving mottled surface-texture of what seems like very small crystalline fragments. It then cuts to a spinning black silhouette shape of what looks like a drawing pin, which is joined by moving shapes of nails. This section is repeated in negative – white shapes against a black background – after a section of again surface-texture, but more painterly and less definable in terms of what it is. And then a brief hand-written French word appears, too brief to read. There follows an extremely brief shot of what seems like a street lamp moving across the top of the frame from right to left, followed by rotating circular figures arrayed roughly in lines. It then cuts to a night shot of street lights and what seems like a funfair roundabout, rhyming the previous white shapes against the black background. At a first viewing the rapid contiguity of shots with their fairly abstract shapes means that when camera photography is used it takes a moment to realise it. The distinction between shots of real things and those of shapes achieved by printing methods is fudged.

Although *Return to Reason* is renowned as a fairly arbitrarily structured film in the Dada spirit, there are nevertheless strong unifying aspects to it. One is its movement, a fast-moving rhythm within the frame set up by these various shots. The switch from the photograms to the night scenes of lights stresses these similarities through the formal property of movement, and of shapes moving on a flat, 'neutral', background. Man Ray is thus establishing formal patterns among disparate material. The film steadily includes more real-camera-based shots – of a revolving kinetic sculpture and notably of a nude torso, again treated through light and negative pho-togram-like techniques.

Surrealism

The 1920s produced very little by way of a *surrealist cinema*. In fact, Surrealism has produced few films within its central tradition. Ironically, its influence had been felt most on mainstream film, art cinema and advertising, much to the discomfort of its more purist practitioners. The 'true' surrealist film-makers are to be counted on one hand – Luis Buñuel, Jacques Brunius, Jan Svankmajer, Joseph Cornell (see Hammond 1991). The early surrealists were obsessed by cinema but largely as a massive receptacle of found objects – film narratives, their *mise-en-scènes* and their 'stars'. It can be argued that their strongest impulse was not to make films but to experience them and to marvel at mainly Hollywood's naïveté, its extraordinary expressions of innocence, desire and mad love – in other words, its very unconscious. In this spirit, surrealist film literature of the 1920s and 1930s is a celebration (of Fantomas, Keaton, Krazy Kops, serials) of an already-given cinema.

Luis Buñuel and Salvador Dali: Un Chien Andalou

However, one film stands out in the decade as one of the most influential films ever – Buñuel and Dali's *Un Chien Andalou* (1928) (see Kovacs 1980; Buñuel 1984). More problematically, for this book, it was a film that, according to Dali, 'ruined in a single evening ten years of pseudo-intellectual post-war avant-gardism' (quoted in Sitney 1979: 3). Surrealism was a highly conscious and well-orchestrated attack on bourgeois culture, of which early modernism and the avant-gardes are seen as a part, abstraction especially – 'Mr Mondrian's lozenges'. Yet *Un Chien Andalou* proved popular with that very bourgeois class, a fact pointed out to Buñuel and Dali by fellow surrealists on its first very successful screening (Buñuel 1984: 108).

Interestingly, *Un Chien Andalou* was made at the beginning of Buñuel's involvement with Surrealism and to that extent had no model except for Dulac's *The Seashell and the Clergyman* and Man Ray's films. But *Un Chien Andalou*'s more likely influences are the montage films of Eisenstein and its devices (slow motion, super-imposition), perhaps the more conservative French impressionist avant-garde with their super-impositions and heightened moments (after all Buñuel had worked for a few years as an assistant to Jean Epstein before making *Un Chien Andalou*), plus the avant-garde films Buñuel had programmed himself in the 1920s.

Earlier films with Dada tendencies like Clair's *Entr'acte* or Murphy and Leger's *Ballet Mecanique*, while containing elements of parody, skit and irreverence, had none of the hard-edged subversion of *Un Chien Andalou*. The latter's concern is neither with *form* nor spontaneous fun, and despite its makers' assertion that it was simply an illogical narrative culled from their dreams, it is usually experienced as a highly controlled and, in some sense, coherent work. This is not to say that it is easily interpreted. Like many successful art works it eludes reductive analysis, yet it is all of a piece in a way in which a film like *Entr'acte* is not. It is definitely not an experiment, nor formal exploration, nor an off-the-cuff broadside.

Un Chien Andalou begins with the intertitle 'Once upon a time...' and a lively tango soundtrack (see Drummond 1977; Williams 1981) and then a medium close-up of a hand holding a strap while the other sharpens a cut-throat razor. A close-up follows of a man (Buñuel himself) with a cigarette dangling from the corner of his mouth, looking down and standing in front of what seem to be curtain drapes. Then there is a cut, back to the hands, which now stop sharpening the razor and test its sharpness by slicing a fingernail. It cuts back to the face looking down at this action. There is then a medium shot of the man with the razor standing in front of a window. He turns and opens the window and squeezes through the space to exit, followed by a cut to a medium shot of the man coming out onto a balcony at what seems night, with deep shadows and a strong light on the wall on the right of the screen. It cuts to a medium head-shoulders shot of the man with a cigarette still in his mouth, looking slowly up to the sky. There is a shot of the moon. It cuts back to the same shot of the man looking up followed by another shot of the moon and then a shot of the man looking up. There is then a close-up of a woman's face looking into camera. A hand of someone (a man) standing behind her comes into screen right to open one of her eyes wider. His other hand comes across the screen and holds the razor over her eye. It cuts to the moon as a thin horizontal cloud passes across it. Then follows an extreme close-up of the eye as the razor slices through it.

This shot breakdown of the film's first sequence reveals its unified space and time until the sudden appearance of the woman. This unexpected presence contrasts with the sequence's preceding conventional build up around the figure of the man. A further strange feature of the scene is the suggestion that the man wielding the razor at the beginning is not the same as the man who slices the woman's eye. The latter is wearing a tie (striped like the enigmatic box), whereas the other man has an open-necked shirt. Thus the more obvious disjuncture created by the woman's sudden appearance is deepened by the ambiguity around the male figure. Are there two men, or is there a break in time?

If there are two men then the eye-slicing action could be the content of the first man's musing or fantasy or memory. One could push it further and argue that the entire film after the man's glance at the moon was a reverie of sorts. The fact that the first man is played by Buñuel could support the idea of the film as subjective, possibly autobiographical. What upsets this view is the presence of intertitles between sequences, suggesting a more objective viewpoint.

The sequence sets up the violent tone of the rest of the film, and its link between sex and aggression; a sort of sadistic impulse runs throughout. A romantic sensibility is also implicated at the film's core with the bold visual match between the cloud 'slicing' the moon and the razor literally slicing the eye. It implies an identity between nature and consciousness and action. Furthermore, the surrealist enthusiam for such dream states or reveries is a development of the nineteenth-century romantic version of the same states as Buñuel probably recognised (his choice of the Wagner soundtrack supports this and should not be treated too ironically).

Ambiguity and symbolism abound in the film as does a more conventional construction of time and space – as in the sequence of the woman reading in the room. This begins with a deep-space shot of a fairly large bourgeois room with large windows, in which a woman sits reading at a table. There is a dissolve to a medium shot of her. She looks up, startled, as if she has heard something (what could that be – a bicycle through closed windows?). It cuts to a shot of a man (a third man?) on a bicycle crossing left to right of screen; cut back to the woman who tosses the book aside. There is then an insert shot of her book opened at the Vermeer painting, *The Lacemaker*. The film cuts to the woman standing up, looking determined and then crossing to the windows right of screen; cut to her approaching the windows from screen right. She looks out and flinches. There is a cut to what she sees: the man cycling on the street below. Return to the shot of the woman who looks out once more and then steps back again. The film cuts to a shot of the cycling man who stops by slowing down and simply falling over onto the ground. It then cuts back to the woman standing back from the window, shocked and uttering something at this bizarre act. She then returns to the window. There follows a shot of the man from the opposite angle, lying part on the street and part on the pavement, but still on his bicycle. It cuts back to the woman saying something as she looks through the window, followed by a medium shot from behind her (with the bed to the left of the window), as she turns to cross the room. It cuts to a medium shot of her crossing the room, moving with her as she opens the door and exits. Cut back to a medium shot of the man lying with a diagonal striped bag around his neck, as he stares off to screen right. Cut to the apartment door opening and she exits and descends the stairs out of the bottom of the shot. There is a cut to a shot of the prostrate man now looking in a different direction, followed by a shot of the apartment block's main entrance and the woman coming out and standing, hands clasped anxiously. She moves towards the man. It cuts to her bent next to him covering his face in kisses. A close-up of the striped bag being opened and a cloth-wrapped object being taken out is followed by a cut to the woman doing this inside a room.

While much is made of the deeper meaning of *Un Chien Andalou*, there is a sense in which its meaning and its mystery lie as much in its 'surface' happenings and details as they do in any Freudian reading. The consciously intended aspects of the films are undervalued as ways of understanding our responses to it.

There are inexplicable aspects to this sequence. For example, it seems as if the woman is expecting the man; her tender kisses and caresses when she reaches him fallen on the pavement would seem to support this. She is initially angry with him – but why? Because of his strange feminine attire and then his (stupid?) falling over? Or both? The film shows her saying things we cannot hear. Her hearing him in the first place is perplexing; for how and what can she hear in a room high up from a busy road, of a fairly noiseless cyclist?

What is clear from this shot breakdown is how much of the editing of these early sequences of the films is conventional. Buñuel makes much use of the shot/reverse shot format. The man looks up and the cut is to what he sees. Buñuel edits a series of shots (back shot, p.o.v. of the road ahead, side shot and repeats of these) of the man cycling, which gives us, in a fairly conventional way, his general direction and establishes the length of the journey. The cuts between the woman looking out of the window and at what she sees (the cycling man and his fall) are fairly standard shots of looks and what is being looked at, and repeated in order to gather dramatic weight and tension to the scene. Similarly, Buñuel cuts to get people across rooms and out of doors (e.g. two shots, the last one moving with the woman as she leaves to attend to the stricken man in the street, to get the woman from the window to outside her apartment). He picks her up, exiting and descending the interior stairs, and then again cuts to the front door and her coming out onto the front steps. Buñuel was never to indulge in the arty shot; there is always a rather simple straightforwardness to his framing, composition and editing.

For Buñuel, *Un Chien Andalou*'s subject-matter was passion, but highly articulated. And for all its irrational zeal, it is a strongly moral film. Buñuel's world is our world. Compared with *Emak Bakia*'s (1926) stream of consciousness, *Un Chien Andalou* is a highly crafted unified drama. What for Dali was a critique of modern society, was for Buñuel – through the use of dream material as its source – an expression of pure desire, or instinctual demands (the Freudian id), the often-destructive passion of the surrealist 'mad love'. *Un Chien Andalou* was a joint project although Buñuel directed it – both artists in a common spirit of *irrational production* only accepting ideas they both agreed on. This sensibility was identified by Buñuel as in the lineage of Romanticism in this case filtered through Surrealism. This Romanticism characterises *Un Chien Andalou*'s very opening sequence with its mysterious partly-female-clothed cycling man accompanied by Wagner's *Tristan und Isolde*.

If Dada had been the original anti-art movement, then Surrealism was to hammer into shape the former's iconoclasm using social, political and psychological theories culled from the revolutionary undercurrents of the post-war years. The Soviet Union was a prime source (although the surrealists were to split along the Stalinist/Trotskyist fault-line) as were Freud's radical theories of the unconscious and sexuality. As Buñuel was well aware, some of the revolutionary fervour was no more than one faction of the bourgouisie (surrealists) turning viciously on its own kind. Freud's theories were also in the air in cultural and art circles and Buñuel and Dali were familiar with them at the time they began making films together.

Un Chien Andalou has a dramatic structure rather than a narrative one, though Buñuel inserts mock illogical 'narrative' intertitles. The film is a series of both ordinary and bizarre events whose dramatic and shock qualities derive from their realist rendition but which have no narrative cause, source or logic. The opening sequence is a clear example of this. But in many ways the surrealists were right to understand themselves as fundamentally opposed to the avant-garde of the time. Buñuel's move to mainstream art cinema is no accident but rather the direction to which *Un Chien Andalou* was already pointing. It is not an anti-narrative film but one that plays with narrative. Interestingly, the irrational impulse of Man Ray is closer to the subjectivist strand of modernism which emerges fully-fledged in action painting and Stan Brakhage's films of post-World War Two America. The search for self-authenticity is not paramount in surrealist work as it is in Dada.

The European film avant-garde of the 1920s was truly innovative. Many of its concerns – abstraction, improvisational free-flowing image-making, image and text, social critique, dream reveries – have had a continuing influence. It not only laid down markers for future aesthetic strategies but also for cultural and political opposition. And as we shall see in the next chapter, when this avant-garde is joined by the film experiments of the budding new state of the Soviet Union, the claim of the 1920s to being the great and defining period of the twentieth-century avant-gardes is fully substantiated.

3   THE 1920s: SOVIET EXPERIMENTS

The Soviet Union in the 1920s was *the* centre of avant-garde film – Sergei
Eisenstein, Dziga Vertov, Lev Kuleshov, Vsevolod Pudovkin and Alexander
Dohvchenko being its foremost figures for international cineastes. The
Soviet experiment was supreme: partly for its political revolutionary context mirroring and shaping the ideals of many intellectuals and workers,
partly for its ambitions – a cinema engaging with the most important social
issues of the day – in a way which did not reduce them to star-studded
melodramas but acted out on a huge canvas of social and political sweep,
and partly for its exciting new forms. There had been no such phenomenon on such a scale at that time nor has there been since in cinema. As
a model, the Soviet cinema blended political idealism, heroic nationhood
and artistic achievement in a heady concoction. This was an avant-garde
active on a huge international scale and not restricted to the narrow con-
fines of the art world (see Gillespie 2000).

   This influential film experiment was running parallel to the West
European avant-gardes. By the 1930s its leading light, Sergei Eisenstein,
was a world-wide phenomenon, lauded and lionised even in the 'enemy
camp' of America's capitalist Hollywood (Bordwell 1993). It is difficult to
overestimate the impact of his films and personality on cinema and his
fellow film-makers. With only a handful of films (albeit feature-length)
– *Strike* (1925), *Battleship Potemkin* (1926), *October* (1927) – made in
rapid succession, he combined a heroic radical form – montage – with

political revolutionary aims. Crucially, he was also a prolific film theorist. For Buñuel, *Battleship Potemkin* 'was the most beautiful film in the history of the cinema' (1984: 88). But like Buñuel, Eisenstein was unimpressed by the formalist tricks of the French and German avant-garde, reserving his admiration only for Leger's *Ballet Mecanique* and Ruttmann's poetic documentary *Symphony for a City* (1927).

Though seen as avant-garde at the time, Eisenstein raises interesting issues around the notion. For instance, there is a substantial differ-ence between his ambitions and attitude to film and those of the West Europeans like Man Ray, Richter, Ruttmann *et al.* Eisenstein deals with narrative. His films are historical and political dramas however much they are distinct in their methods to those of Hollywood, especially in the Soviet director's rejection of singular heros and heroines. From the perspective of the abstract painter Malevich, Eisenstein and Vertov were both guilty of not exploiting and developing in film the progress made by early modern-ism in the visual arts. For Malevich both film-makers remained within the clutches of drama and ideological content. Pointedly, Malevich turned to Hans Richter when he thought of developing a film project. Thus we have a sense of the complexities of the modernism movement sweeping through Europe in the 1920s.

Another way of understanding this is to articulate the difference between Eisenstein and the European avant-gardes not simply in terms of form and politics, but also in the former's emotional expression. Eisenstein wanted to communicate his passions to the audience – the disgust, horror and outrage felt at the old system and the hope, joy and exuberance for the new. Eisenstein's unflinching desire for a mass audience encouraged his perennial search for a psychological theory of how film emotionally engaged the spectator. Interestingly, the British avant-garde film-maker and writer Malcolm Le Grice's rejection of Eisenstein is for the latter's 'expressive narrative' (1977: 59).

As we know from his writings and life, Eisenstein was genuinely inter-ested in and sympathetic to many Hollywood directors, including John Ford, Charlie Chaplin and Walt Disney, as he was to the European art cinema of P. W. Pabst, Carl Theodor Dreyer and Fritz Lang. He was critical of formalist cinema, quarrelling with his fellow director Dziga Vertov's 'formalist jackstraws?' (Eisenstein 1949: 43) and demanding 'kino-fist' rather than 'kino-eye' from cinema. By this, Eisenstein understood his cinema as a call to action or at least an identification with the emotions necessary for class struggle, emotions he hoped to arouse in the spectator through his 'montage of attractions' (see Eisenstein 1988).

Despite his own antipathy to the label, Eisenstein's avant-garde credentials were based on his formal experimentalism and radical social and political aims. For some, it is this merging of radical form and content (or signifier with signified) that identifies avant-gardism at its most successful and most potent (see Hess & Ashbery 1967). Annette Michelson (1966) identifies Eisenstein as being examplary of this 'radical inspiration'. But Eisenstein is firmly in a realist tradition. There is none of Vertov's perceptual distortion. Even if his *mise-en-scène* and compositional proclivities are highly stylised this only places him in a spectrum with Hollywood filmmakers – not qualitatively different, and hence his success in the bastion of capitalist film-making.

A further question that is raised by reference to Eisenstein's case is: avant-garde of what? The military-based concept of a vanguard implies a main body following in its tracks. In the history of cinema, Eisenstein can lay most claim to being a vanguard artist of the mainstream and commercial art cinema, his work being acknowledged as such by Hollywood, and influencing it (in the work of Hitchcock for example). On the other hand, Hollywood was indifferent to avant-garde film. Eisenstein's writings are not fundamentally at odds with Hollywood narrative cinema. In comparison, avant-garde film-makers are either indifferent to the mainstream or treat it as anathema. There is an ambivalence in fact in the attitudes of many vanguard film-makers to Hollywood throughout the 1920s and 1930s. As we shall see it is only in the postwar period that a more sustained and widely shared revulsion for Hollywood became common to avant-garde film-makers.

The 'montage' method was at the centre of Eisenstein's work. It had an enormous impact on cinema style. It has been seen as so fundamental that it is the other half of a basic duality understood in cinema – the other being realism. Nevertheless, it is an elusive notion even in Eisenstein's own work and writings. It was also shared by most of the Soviet film-makers in some form or another. Its stress was on editing, not new in film-making, of course, as Griffiths had shown, yet here editing was not simply a means of articulating a story but was a dynamic practice in its own right. Of course an edit implies an image on either side of it; in Eisenstein's early aesthetic this connecting of images was seen as a moment of jarring, of harsh and vivid juxtaposition aimed at shocking, at overwhelming the spectator.

Later, montage became a means of suggesting a subtle complexity of meanings, as in certain sequences in *October*, where it is used most successfully. At other times in Eisenstein's films it is used in a rhythmic musical sense to establish an emotional expressive pace to a sequence and also to accentuate the graphic compositions of the shots so joined together. It is in this latter sense of the term that montage has had most influence on film-making, mainstream and avant-garde, since then.

'Montage' sequences from October

October was commissioned for the tenth anniversary of the Russian Revolution, and Eisenstein stated that there were parts of the film which were 'purely experimental' and that it used 'new and difficult methods'. Following *Battleship Potemkin* and *Strike* it was the director's third feature film. The film depicts the February 1917 'bourgeois' revolution and the setting up of the provisional government which was overthrown, in turn, by Lenin's revolutionary Bolsheviks in October of the same year. In Eisenstein's hands this dramatic historical period is mythologised by exaggerations, distortions, evasions and a grand monumental style which has become almost like a document of the events themselves. But it is an acted story of those events told with all the energetic and assertive confidence and brilliance of Eisenstein's montage method. In many ways *October* mirrors what John Ford (admired by Eisenstein), perhaps less consciously, was doing for America in his westerns and with the same respect for mythology. To this extent it is a moral film insofar as socialist values take precedence over strict historical truth.

Let us examine two famous sequences as examples of Eisenstein's experimental method. They also exemplify different modes of montage used by him in the film. The short sequence (within a slightly longer one known as the 'July Days')[1] begins with rapid machine-gun fire aimed at the demonstrating crowds. As they attempt to escape across the bridge a young woman is shot down, as is a horse drawing a carriage. Both fall across the bridge divide and as it is raised the horse comes to hang high above the river until it plunges into it. It is a brilliantly edited sequence in which time is both elongated and repeated, and in which movement in the frame counterpoints editing rhythms and nineteenth-century symbolism jostles with constructivist patterns and movements.

Two powerful modes of expression are contrasted in this sequence – the modernist and the symbolist – each stressing the other's characteristics. The fallen woman's long hair straddles the bridge divide and as the bridge is raised her hair is delicately drawn along it, contrasting vividly and with pathos, the dead girl's long soft vibrant hair with the hard mechanical bridge divide and its upward movement as the hair falls slowly in the opposite direction. The girl is strongly associated visually with the collapsing horse whose legs are painfully spread-eagled as it falls.

As the bridge opens, the dead white horse lying next to the girl hangs over the edge of the inexorably rising bridge, counterbalanced by the carriage it is still attached to. The horse cruelly and precariously hangs until the bridge almost reaches its full opening when it falls with an enormous splash into the river below. As the bridge and horse rise, Eisenstein cuts back and forth to the strong graphic lines of the bridge's metal structure, it too moving slowly. It is as if all of humanity is caught and broken and killed by these huge abstract structures, moving mechanically and crushing and dragging all before it. It is a strong symbol of the duality of machine and body, state and citizen, history and agent, male and female, oppressed and oppressor, life and death.

The dead white horse is a traditional symbol of the apocalypse in Russian culture. Similarly the dead girl with her long hair is an equally traditional symbol of innocence, virtue and victimhood. Again, she, like the horse, in this sequence is imbricated in the huge soulless metal structures of the modern age. This is a remarkable example of Eisenstein's ability to marry two opposing aesthetic sensibilities – the modernist and symbolist – into a resonant image of both Marxist determinism and Romantic fatalism. Here is 'montage' as a form of metaphorical 'editing'. In many ways one can rethink his montage method as a solution to a mode of symbolist image construction one in which an aesthetic saturation of the image leaves no means of connecting shots through the usual means of narrative (Cavell 1979; O'Pray 1993).

The vulnerable body as victim depicted within rigid graphic material structures is a continuing visual motif in his work – one thinks of the child held by its feet and then dropped by the horseman in the worker's tenements in *Strike* (a similar image is found in *Alexander Nefsky* [1938]); or the young handsome boy-Czar standing beneath the showering sparkling coins at his coronation in *Ivan the Terrible Part 1* (1944). The whole of the latter film is shot under the influence of this aesthetic. Its compositions construct humans contorted and repressed by a looming overbearing architecture and claustrophobic shadows of its interiors. This aesthetic becomes a strong trait within the succeeding avant-garde, notably in the film work of Kenneth Anger, Maya Deren, Gregory Markopolous and Derek Jarman.

It is close to a late nineteenth-century decadence which would have been familiar to Eisenstein. He never embraces any kind of full-blown constructivism of the kind we find in Vertov's *Man With a Movie Camera* (1929). This symbolist trait also explains Eisenstein's continued popularity with a broad cinema audience who recognised such universal symbols and themes.

As a whole, Eisenstein's work comprises impacted poetic passages of a cold sadistic austerity in which awesome mechanical structures – both architectural and filmic – overwhelm and crush the human agent. In this sense Eisenstein is more profoundly anti-humanist than a clear-cut constructivist like Vertov (see Michelson 1984; Petric 1987). It is no accident that many of his most impressive sequences deal with such a cold, mechanical sadism as in the execution of the babies sequence in *Alexander Nefsky* and in the formation of the German knights in which his compositional strengths are most apparent in a film in which his aesthetic is probably at its weakest.

Dziga Vertov

Vertov's films are usually described as constructivist and hence modernist in their sensibility. Not only do they exemplify a constructivist visual style but they are largely documentaries – films about the contemporary Soviet Union, dedicated to celebrating not the historical forces which led to the Russian Revolution but the daily life of the country and its inhabitants.

Vertov has most influenced avant-garde film-makers; his rejection of the dramatic narrative has suited many contemporary film-makers. His formalist 'tricks' have also appealed by their abstract nature across cultural and ideological divides. His love of the mundane and everyday has appealed to the microcosmic viewpoint that has inspired many avant-gardists. Vertov's revolutionary left-wing politics to which his films paid service were also appealing to the 1970s New Left European experimental film-makers, and Godard's adoption of Vertov's name for his left-wing production unit in the late 1960s marks this identification with him.

Eisenstein is seen as too bombastic, too manipulative in the interests of ideological narratives either seen as politically alien or, these days, as politically anachronistic. Vertov's marginalisation by the Soviet authorities after the early 1930s – after which he worked irregularly on newsreels until his death in 1954 – also fulfils some of the romance of the avant-garde.

For many on the Left, especially post-Godard of the late 1960s, Vertov occupied the moral high ground over Eisenstein. After the de-Stalinisation of the European Left, Vertov's experimental documentaries – like *Man With a Movie Camera*, *One Sixth of the Earth* (1926) and *Enthusiasm* (1930) – have been embraced largely for their documentary novelty as well as a poetic montage aesthetic. In the 1930s, for example, Vertov's reputation among the European avant-garde was overshadowed by that of Eisenstein. Jay Leyda describes *Man With a Movie Camera* as an 'avant-garde' film but also recognises its paradoxical nature as a film 'produced by VUFKU, a state trust' (1973: 252).

Man With a Movie Camera

The film's opening credits hail this as an 'experiment in cinematic communication of visible events without the aid of intertitles' and as an 'experimental work that aims at creating a truly international absolute language'.[2]
It is more than a city symphony. This is a language reminiscent of the
European avant-garde in Germany, influenced by the innovation in painting. In the same vein, Vertov's cinema has been described and treated as
'constructivist' although it is in that aesthetic where it reconstructs reality
as did Lissitsky or Rodchenko as opposed to a purely abstract constructivist mode.

It is also a celebration of the modern as much as of the revolutionary.
With its obsession with machines, speeding cars and bikes, radio, outdoor
sports, street magicians and the more rudely vulgar – women's breasts – it
parallels the rush of the modern into futurism, cubism and Dada. Finally,
it is subtitled 'The Diary of a Cameraman', who was Mikhail Kaufman,
Vertov's brother, whom we see throughout the film carrying the camera
and filming (Vertov's wife Elizaveta Svilova was the editor). Of course,
there is also another cameraman filming Kaufman!

The trickery of the fairground and seaside side-show is given its modern technological expression in the film's own humorous special-effects
– a 'magic show'. To this extent the film is more modern than anything
made by Eisenstein who usually had his eye on the high-art tradition. Even
Vertov's traditional Russian dance is performed by a fashionably bob-cut
young dancer. In fact women are centrally portrayed in his film and one
suspects not for simple political reasons but for sexual ones too.[3] The film
has an intensely democratic form and subject-matter. Its view of Soviet
culture stemming more from the *proletkult* than Eisenstein's more authori-
tarian and traditional references: the camera as a gun.[4]

But in the end Vertov is observing culture in its broadest means
of production and reception. But perhaps this where Vertov and Stan
Brakhage, compared to Eisenstein, share an apolitical goal: perception
as revolutionary act. For Vertov and Brakhage, the social context of such a
radical perception is perhaps of a secondary matter. Eisenstein's work is

Figure 2 *Man With a Movie Camera* (Dziga Vertov, 1929)

much more revolutionary in its traditional party-politics sense. His notion of class struggle, while fairly crude, is nevertheless well-marked in his films. For Vertov, in *Man With a Movie Camera*, this is less so and explains Eisenstein's jibes of 'formalist jackstraws'. *Man With a Movie Camera* is also a film which seeks to include its own labours and process as part of the general economic production, memorably as the cameraman with his Debrie camera on his shoulders passes a stooping miner on his way to the coalface in the underground pit tunnels.

Man With a Movie Camera is a *tour de force* and even today its excitement, energy, audacity and craft captivates. It is one of the great poetic achievements of the cinema. The addition of music (which Vertov always intended) in the recent video/DVD release of the film has also brought out its more irreverent fun side (the older generation generally saw and studied it as a silent film, leaving a potentially misleading feeling of high seriousness and perhaps dourness which the music soundtrack immediately erases). The music also underlines its structure, with definite periods of quiet, agitated rhythm, seriousness, slapstick and lyricism. Music also signals the beginnings, ends and climaxes of sequences.

The film is of the projection of the film which we see and is bracketed between a sequence showing the audience arriving at the cinema and beginning to watch the film and at the end, the end of the film in the cinema. It is, in other words, an attempt to show the filming of the film, its editing and eventual projection – the production and consumption process (but not its economics, for example).

As a film, it is one of complex visual patterns and rhythms – of film image, of nature, of machines, of actions, of social behaviour, of bodies. It is also one of rhymes and metaphors and of the film-maker as a magician (revealing his tricks). It is in the film's inseparable aspects of graphic forms, editing and visual semantics that it stands apart. But it is also a brilliant collection of images of reality, a property of the film sometimes buried in the idea that meaning is appropriated in such films simply by the relationships between shots and not of what the shots are of. It is, after all, this realism (a cinema of facts) that Vertov wished to assert against Eisenstein's storytelling (see Cavell 1979). It also places the camera as the 'hero' of the film, and by implication the film-makers themselves, although it sometimes animates the camera so that it seems to have a life of its own – an autonomous seer – in shots of it as a many-legged giant looming over the city. Indeed, it is so rich that choosing an extract for analysis is difficult. We will look at one sequence in the leisure section of the film, in which Vertov intercuts between men racing motorbikes on a circuit and young women on a fair merry-go-round.

Even in such a fairly straightforward sequence, the levels of visual and graphic meaning are subtle. At a broad level, the men are moving through their own controlled active use of machines (motorbikes) around a circular track; the women on the other hand are being passively moved in a similar circular movement by a machine not in their control. So gender is divided along notions of passivity and activity in relation to machines (motorbike and merry-go-round). At a more individual level, the men are rigid and purposeful and concentrated on their activity of riding the bike whereas the women are relaxed and smiling at their own pleasure and at the crowds watching them. In a wonderful shot, one of the women overtly relaxes her body and leans against the merry-go-round pole eating a sweet with an expression of complacent luxuriousness, contrasted immediately with the bodily rigidity and anonymity of the motorbike men.

This intercutting between the motorbike circuit and merry-go-round also includes very brief shots of athletes jumping and at the moment of landing, perhaps contrasting movement under one's own bodily means as opposed to the mechanical means of movement of the two main activities. In both cases, point-of-view shots are given from Kaufman's camera, seen in one shot mounted on his handlebars, and from what seem the women's point of view of the crowds gathered at the edge of the fast moving merry-go-round, blurred by the speed of the merry-go-round.

Without doubt we can also discern a sexual component to the sequence – the aggressive controlled activity of the men and the passive, relaxed openness of the women. At the graphic level there are different kinds of shots – the high camera tracing the visual patterns of the bikes on the circuit; the medium shot capturing the facial and bodily expression of the women on the merry-go-round; the point-of-view shots with their blurred dizzy instabilty. Equally in the motorbike shots the camera is moving with the bikes, but on the merry-go-round the camera is moving with the ride.

The Soviet 'experiment' overshadowed nearly all else. Its own ambiguity towards the avant-garde had little effect on its influence on later avant-garde film-makers – as varied as Stan Brakhage, Peter Gidal and Jean-Luc Godard. To state the obvious, much of its ongoing influence lies in its central role in a real revolutionary situation. Unlike West European film-makers whose work gestured towards change, reform and even revolution, the Soviet film-makers had to deal with its reality. More interestingly, the Soviet film-makers were part of a fairly large monolithic State film industry and not working as individual artisans. They were also aiming at mass audiences (however successful that was in reality) and not simply at other artists and intellectuals or the advanced elements of the bourgeoisie.

The reasons for the collapse of the Soviet avant-garde are complex. To some extent, energies ran out by the end of the 1920s and beginning of the 1930s; the Soviet State in the early 1930s turned to socialist realism and spurned what it called 'formalism'. And, of course, there was the arrival of sound, which meant that what had been a primarily visual approach had to contend with what was inevitably a strengthening of film's realism with the addition of sound. The addition of sound in film also helped to loosen the ties with the 'silent' visual fine arts.

1   For a fuller description of the entire seqeunce see D. Bordwell (1993) *The Cinema of Eisenstein*. London: Harvard University Press, 86–9.
2   Yuri Tsivian's excellent commentary on the BFI video/DVD of the film is a mandatory tool for understanding the film.
3   The new (and contemporarily up-beat) soundtrack supports a more light-hearted approach to the film which by no means undermines its sheer audacity and seriousness.
4   It is a socio-political precursor of Brakhage. It is no accident that it contains a sequence of Brakhagian-like subjectivity, as it provides a view from the blinking moving eye. Comparing *Anticipation of the Night* (1958) with this sequence we can perhaps recognise Brakhage's struggle to establish a personal style out of that technique.

4 THE 1920s AND 1930s: BRITISH AVANT-GARDE FILM

The link between this chapter and the last is direct: the massive influence of the Soviet film experiment, especially of Eisenstein's, on British film vanguardism in the 1920s and 1930s.[1] Film avant-gardes proliferated in this period in many countries (see Curtis 1971; Le Grice 1977; Christie 1998) including America (Horak 1995), Belgium, Netherlands (Dusinberre 1979), Poland (Rees 1993–94) and Czechoslovakia (Hames 1995).

The innovative and relatively well-known work of Len Lye, Humphrey Jennings and Norman McLaren produced within the terrain of the documentary movement has tended to overshadow a broader experimental film community which stretched back to the 1920s. This loose grouping contributed not only films – some lost, many neglected – but also a cultural framework for a complex web of film practices ranging from avant-garde experiments to agit-prop.

In Britain in the 1920s, film was seen largely as a vulgar populist medium; it had not been embraced by the English intelligentsia. It made its cultural impact in the late 1920s with a generation who were largely introduced to art cinema and educated into thinking seriously about film by the influential Film Society and film journal *Close Up* (founded in 1925 and 1927 respectively). Through the Film Society audiences encountered the films of Eisenstein, Vertov, Pabst, Lang, Richter, Dreyer and many others for the first time. Through *Close Up*, they became familiar with the theories of Vertov, Pudovkin and especially Eisenstein. For example, Basil Wright speaks of being 'acutely aware of the Russian Manifesto' on sound cinema (it was published in *Close Up* in 1928) when embarking on documentary film-making in the early 1930s (1974: 114). Both Eisenstein and Vertov visited London and showed their films in the late 1920s and early 1930s.

What little film experimentation took place in the 1920s was often on the fringe of the mainstream industry – as is testified by the work of Adrian Brunel, Ivor Montagu and Sinclair Hill, who all forged careers in commercial cinema. Like many others they were enthralled by fashionable avant-garde ideas of German expressionist film and Soviet montage, the result both of visits abroad by some British film-makers and of the Film Society's programmes. These visual ideas were also successfully incorporated into the films of Alfred Hitchcock, for example *The Ring* (1927).

The Film Society was based initially in London and supported by leading progressive intellectuals, politicians, scientists and the still influential Bloomsbury group in the figures of Virginia Woolf, John Maynard Keynes, Clive Bell and Roger Fry. Conceived by Ivor Montagu and the actor Hugh Miller as they returned from Berlin in 1925 (see Montagu 1980), it was inspired by the European film clubs and modelled on the Stage Society which had been set up in 1899 to show dramatists whose plays were otherwise unavailable to English audiences. Similarly, one of the Film Society's prime functions was to make European art cinema available in Britain. But it provided a crucial cultural space for viewing not only European art films by Pabst, Eisenstein, Pudovkin and others, but also experimental abstract works by Richter, Ruttmann and Fischinger. It enjoyed enormous popularity and prestige, influencing both the avant-garde and, surprisingly, the commercial cinema (see Samsom 1986).

The Society also provided financing for the young artist Len Lye's *Tusalava* (1929), a black-and-white film heavily influenced by his experiences of Maori art and modernist abstraction. The Film Society also organised study groups, notably one led by Eisenstein. In 1929 Hans Richter ran such a group involving Eisenstein which produced the left-wing film *Everyday* (completed and soundtrack added in 1969).[2]

The journal *Close Up* broadly supported 'advanced guard' film and art cinema although those distinctions were not at the time as fixed as they were to become. It was edited by Kenneth Macpherson and Bryher, the nom de plume of Annie Winifred Ellerman, the daughter of an enormously wealthy shipping magnate who was thought to be the richest man in England at his death in 1933. Bryher's money financed *Close Up*.

Founded in English literary modernism, *Close Up* was aligned to Bloomsbury, and through Bryher to the Sitwell's poetic axis of 1920s English cultural life. In a letter to Gertrude Stein, Macpherson describes the magazine as 'dealing with films from the artistic, psychological and educational points of view' (1998: 14). It published a variety of writings including essays by Dorothy Richardson, classic theoretical texts by Eisenstein, Freudian film analysis by Barbara Low and Hans Sachs, summaries of national cinemas, debates on race in cinema and on censorship; pleas for independent film production and distribution; critiques of Hollywood and the British commercial cinema; and celebrations of film stars. It was intensely loyal to the innovative work of Soviet cinema and to the psychological realism of Pabst, understood by them as modernists and thus related to the broader literary modernist movement.

A ground-shift took place in the early 1930s (Bond 1979; Hogenkamp 1986; Baxendale & Pawling 1996). In the late 1920s John Grierson made his influential film *Drifters* (1928), and on the basis of its success he set up a government-sponsored documentary film unit. Grierson surrounded himself with bright young men like Basil Wright, Arthur Elton, Edgar Anstey, Stuart Legg, Paul Rotha and Harry Watt, who breathed the air of social and political idealism (Hynes 1976). This new generation came to film within the moral and political framework associated with that decade's poets and writers – famously Auden, Day Lewis, Spender and Isherwood. They preferred 'the dog-biscuits of EMB [Empire Marketing Board] production to the flesh pots of Elstree and Shepherd's Bush'. In contrast to the light-hearted narrative escapades of Brunel and Montagu, we are brought up short by the action-based approach of Grierson's Empire Marketing Board and subsequently the GPO Film Unit, set up under government patronage (see Hardy 1946: 15).

There was less toleration of the mainstream among this younger generation of film-makers, and at the same time a less self-conscious attitude to ideas of the 'avant-garde', whose aestheticism they also distanced themselves from. It is well to remember that Grierson himself saw the documentary movement as representing 'a reaction from the art world of the early and middle twenties – Bloomsbury, Left Bank, T. S. Eliot, Clive Bell and all' (1998: 116). Of course, 'Bloomsbury' had been supportive of the Film Society, and *Close Up* came from the same literary modernism scene. There was, in other words, a broad move from aestheticism to the politicisation of art, a ground-shift felt across a deeply anxious Europe and reflected, for instance, in Jean Renoir's films.

The urgency felt by film-makers, the impulse to action, not only reflected the politics of the time but also the underlying influence of a Soviet-style commitment shared with early Surrealism. Political and social demands made aesthetics its hand-servant. Oswald Blakeston remembered that he wanted 'to do something quick and magic' (quoted in Dusinberre 1979: 46). Grierson believed that the dedication to the social use of film delivered success where 'other aesthetic and aestheticky movements ... were either fitful or failed'. This can only be a criticism of the work around the *Close Up* group and others of the same ilk. In a similar vein, Paul Rotha describes *Close Up* as 'cultish' (1973: 33).

The 1930s can be seen, with hindsight, to have been the fruitful culmination of the 1920s' passion for film expressed in the work of the Film Society and *Close Up*. Attempts have been made to de-mythologise the decade, to undermine its monolithic presence by pointing to its diverse aesthetics and politics. Different styles and genres jostle against each other as do quite distinct voices, attitudes and political ideologies. But as Samuel Hynes (1976) has remarked, the 1930s is not a decade in which orthodoxy reigned but rather one in which it was worked out.

Such diverse talents as Len Lye, Norman McLaren, Alberto Cavalcanti and Basil Wright blossomed under John Grierson's paternalistic rule at the EMB and then the General Post Office, where British documentary realism was founded (Dusinberre 1980). None of them subscribed to a 'realist' model. Lye was very involved with the modernist avant-garde arts scene of the late 1920s and 1930s while McLaren and Jennings were committed surrealists. Alberto Cavalcanti, brought in by Grierson, was a Paris-based avant-garde film-maker (see Aitken 2000).

Norman McLaren's volatile style is far different to that of Wright and Jennings whose meditations on Englishness (in Jennings' *Spare Time* [1939]) and the Empire (in Wright's *Song of Ceylon* [1934]) suggest quite different sensibilities and interests. By the mid-1930s the internationalist dimension of the British art scene was increased as the émigrés from fascist-threatened Europe began to arrive – for instance László Moholy-Nagy, who made documentaries while in England, and the constructivist Naum Gabo (associated with Stokes, Hepworth and Nicholson and the St Ives avant-garde).

John Grierson: Granton Trawler

Grierson's *Drifters* kick-started the British documentary movement and provided him with enough credit to set up the film unit. His own short EMB film *Granton Trawler* (1934), made some years later, has been overshadowed by the more famous work by Jennings, Cavalcanti and Lye. Grierson shot *Granton Trawler* himself. It was edited by Edgar Anstey and the powerful soundtrack constructed by Cavalcanti (see Aitken 2000: 74–7). It is a superb example of the poetic-montage style influenced by the Soviet school but with its own down-to-earth lyricism distancing it from the wider-embracing monumentality of, say, Vertov's *Enthusiasm* (1930).

The credits come up to the sound of a sea shanty followed by a medium shot of the boat in dock and then a close-up of its prow, followed by a shot of it already at sea. Shadows move across coiled rope on the deck followed by a shot of the captain's body and lower face, but not revealing his eyes. As the wind increases and the images become more dramatic, we hear a sailor whistling, gulls crying and the wind howling. Movement in the frame is provided by the static camera whose motion is determined by the lift and fall of the boat on the heaving sea, which in turn is set against the rise and fall of the sea in the background, with the horizon often at fairly steep angles. This complexity of space and movement adds to the internalistic claustrophobia of the film (it also echoes Vertov's similar use of filming from moving objects). But the movement would be much less effective without the tension that moves between the shifting compositions in the shots and between the shots themselves.

The film's soundtrack was commended at the time. In 1934, the influential art historian Herbert Read admired the way in which the 'impressionistic character of the vocal sounds ... combine with other sounds to produce an asynchronous reinforcement of the visual effect' (quoted in Aitken 2000: 76). It comprises of moaning wind, sea, clanking machinery, creaking ropes and the voices of the seamen. It has a haunting, unsettling quality partially achieved by the obvious disjunction between the visuals and the recorded sound. The men's voices and chit-chat are never shown as synched with the men themselves, creating a distancing quality of a separate aural world in which the slightly unreal quality of the poor recording in fact becomes an aesthetic advantage. Are the voices those of the men in the boat? We assume so but it is never clear. The voices are set against the sound effects creating a dual aural aspect to the film. The visuals have all the monochromatic detail and modeling of light and dark which evokes a time gone by, a distant place already nostalgically recuperated even in the 1930s. The film, in its use of non-sync sound, can also be seen as an example of Grierson's allegiance to the old values of 'silent' cinema.

The general air of romanticism in many British documentaries – for example *Spare Time* (1939) and *Coalface* (1935), despite its modernist chorus – is here unimpeded by any political or social message. Grierson's own suspicion of aestheticism in film is undermined by *Granton Trawler*, perhaps suggesting that what he feared most was his own artistic proclivities and not so much those of others. Having said this, however, there is a rigour in the film which does not turn away from the realities of the working lives he depicts – as, for instance, in the shots of the hard tedious physical labour of gutting the fish and sorting them into baskets on the tilting decks.

The overall perspective is one from the boat with all its attendant movement as it meets rough seas (Anstey's editing conjures up the 'storm'). Grierson's use of the frame here reflects his own view of cinema's 'sensational capacity for enhancing movement ... its abitary rectangle specially reveals movement; it gives it maximum pattern in space and time' (1946:

80). There is a tight, claustrophobic feel to the film. The sky is seen in the background, foregrounded by hovering seagulls, and the sea is always framed by part of the ship – a mast, bow or sides. Most shots of the sea are fairly close-up, often the camera pointed straight into the swelling sea and its heaving waves. This accentuates the graphic dynamics of the shot by flattening out its spatial qualities.

Len Lye

An important context for the avant-garde film in the 1930s was the visual arts. Contemporary artists were divided roughly into three camps – realists, surrealists and constructivists (or abstract artists) – all of whom had an impact on film. There was much overlapping. For example, in 1938 the Artists' International Association organised a debate on the realism versus surrealism issue with William Coldstream (and Graham Bell) on the panel speaking for the former and Humphrey Jennings on the same panel (with Roland Penrose and Julian Trevelyan) speaking for surrealism. Len Lye, a fellow traveller in the surrealist camp, had worked with Jennings on *Birth of a Robot* in 1936 around the time of the infamous Surrealist Exhibition in London. McLaren too was strongly influenced by Surrealism (and revolutionary politics) in his film *Love on the Wing* (1938) with its Freudian free-play. Four of the film-makers who worked with Grierson were painters – Lye, Jennings, McLaren and Coldstream.

Lye has always seemed tangential to the documentarist movement (see Bouhours & Horrocks 2000). A wayward New Zealander who had absorbed modernist experiment and Maori art in relation to painting but with his first film *Tusulava*, funded by the Film Society, began his long artistic trajectory in creating organic shapes and brilliantly controlled and subtle rhythmic expression. The outstanding and indisputable avant-gardist of the British 1930s film movement, Lye provides colour, intense graphic movement and visual pleasure in what at times seemed a rather pedagogical and over-serious artistic climate. It is to Grierson's credit that he both appreciated Lye's talent and found a place for him in the GPO film unit. His first film for Grierson

reveals an opportunistic use of the GPO message (the film was made independently and Grierson asked for a GPO message to be tacked on).
Trade Tattoo

With *Trade Tattoo* (1937), Lye fulfilled his GPO brief without any artistic concession. It is exemplary of the collage technique so prevalent in the 1930s in Europe. Lye uses found-footage (recognisable from other documentary films such as *Night Mail* (1936) and *Coalface*) with his layering of abstract shapes and colours to constantly move the image and colour planes. It is interesting to compare his films with those of the German avant-garde; unlike their outright abstractionism, and formalist tendency, Lye's work stresses the surface and a freer line and brush stroke in his hand-painted work. Much of his painted film work has a wriggling line, or if straight it is often weaving across the screen.

In *Trade Tattoo* Lye merges the two forms of abstraction discussed in Chapter 2. By using found footage treated to optical printing manipulations and overlaying them with separate purely abstract shapes from stencils, Lye both grounds his film in a fleeting but quite focused reality and at the same time helps himself to the imaginative freedom of the abstract stencils. The outcome is quite distinctive, as are the rhythms. For example, rhythms are often expressed by dense columns of simple shapes – circles, ovals – which are in constant individual rhythmic movement but drift towards one or other side of the screen. Thus there is a static multi-pulsation counter-pointed by a slow-moving drifting rhythm. To complicate this even more, a discernible real image of, say, molten metal or a signalling railwayman (usually in negative and tinted) is held in frame as a kind of underlay. All in all, such very short sequences force the eye in a tension of counter-directions.

There is a welcome lack of purism in Lye's mix and match. But at the same time the rigour of the work and its brilliance of execution rarely fails to capture the eye. Animation technique, montage and collage place him alongside the British abstract/constructivist artists of the period such as Henry Moore, Ben Nicholson and Barbara Hepworth.

Britain presents the conundrum of avant-garde work taking place in a

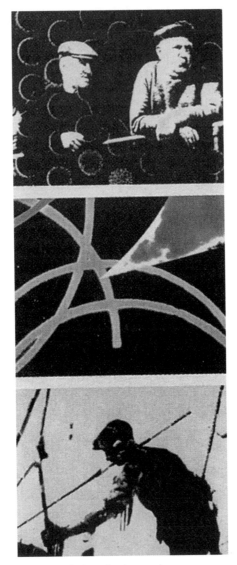

Figure 3 *Trade Tattoo* (Len Lye, 1937)

commercial framework and often with fairly explicit polemical ends. Other film-makers, like Fischinger, had made commercial films in the 1930s, but in the case of Lye his most successful work was in the service of the GPO. His example is cited when aesthetic judgments are made of contemporary television advertising, where experimental forms are used on a par with those found in the avant-garde community itself. In fact, as in the case of Lye and others, contemporary artists like Tony Hill and Chris Cunningham work in both communities. One of the reasons for this is purely economic – a means of earning money for artists who mainly have to rely on fairly meagre rentals – and the other is the resources provided by large advertising budgets to experiment sometimes with the best equipment and technical support.

Deke Dusinberre (1980) has ascribed the centrality of an avant-garde *attitude*, rather than an avant-garde *movement* proper, to this historical moment. He justifiably feels that a fully-fledged avant-garde movement did not really exist, nor were many of the films straightforwardly avant-garde in the way that they were in France and Germany in the 1920s. There was more a general 'avant-garde' attitude shared by the literary modernists of *Close Up* and the radical political inflection of Leftist film-makers like Montagu and Bond. The Film Society's aim to draw the art world into film art was a failure, with the exception, ironically, of Grierson's hard-headed EMB and GPO units, which achieved just that, albeit on a small scale (unlike artists on the continent, Moore, Nicholson, Hepworth and other leading modernists in the 1930s remained resolutely impervious to cinema's charms).

In the end, the inter-war British film avant-garde refuses to be pinned down. Its films, writings and activities are responding to many different needs and demands – formal experimentation cannot be peeled off from social and political subject-matter.

1   Parts of this chapter have been taken from my essay in the booklet accompanying the two video volumes *British Avant-Gardes in the Twenties and Thirties*. London: British Film Institute, 2000.
2   Some influential stalwarts of the Film Society also made films. For example, Ivor Montagu's *Bluebottles*, made in 1928, by way of its scriptwriter, the famous author and progressive H. G. Wells, and two up-and-coming young actors – the husband and wife team of Charles Laughton and Elsa Lanchester.

5   THE 1940s: AMERICAN MYTHOLOGY

The collapse of the avant-gardes in the 1930s in Europe was due to a complexity of factors – internal exhaustion, lack of resource and money, state antagonism and the rise of social-realism in response to burgeoning fascism and Marxist-socialist ideas (see Rees 1999). There was a large exodus of artists from fascism and social unrest in Europe in the 1930s. Avant-garde film-makers Richter, Fischinger, Lye, McLaren and Moholy-Nagy were living in North America by the end of World War Two. Others had moved into different areas of the industry – Cavalcanti was working in the mainstream in Britain, while in the Soviet Union Vertov was demoted to making newsreels. Others had died – Eggeling (in 1925), Ruttmann (1941), Eisenstein (1948), Jennings (1950).

Although there had been experimental film activity in America before the war (see Horak 1995), the post-war period in America heralded the emergence of a clutch of young men and women dedicated to avant-garde film but removed from the Europeans by geography, culture and their relative youth. For them the silent film period was firmly in the past. Film had a history, from whose early years they had no first-hand experience. Importantly they were making film in Hollywood's backyard at the end of its so-called Golden Age. They were not primarily artists dabbling in film but fully committed to the medium. They also had access to some of the classics of the European art cinema and avant-garde through the Art in Cinema film society in San Francisco and Cinema 16 in New York (see MacDonald

2002). Some of them were the product of film-making activities at the San Francisco Art Institute (see Sitney 1979). They included James Broughton, Kenneth Anger, Maya Deren, Willard Maas and Marie Menken, Gregory Markopoulous and Sidney Peterson.

Writing in 1951, Anger attacked the monolithic production processes of commercial cinema which had led to a 'cold' aloof quality, what he called the 'frozen realms' even of the work of those film-makers he admired such as Dreyer, Eisenstein and Robert Bresson (1989: 20). He proclaimed a 'personal cinema' in which expression, improvisation and spontaneity were to be paramount, a poetry of private passions. All of the post-war American avant-garde film-makers mentioned shared these ideals to some degree or other. With the exception of an abstract film strand represented by the Whitney Brothers and Harry Smith, American avant-garde film was dominated in this period by experimental 'narrative' film under the strong influence of Surrealism (Sitney 1974).

It is often argued that the American avant-garde is the direct descendant of the European avant-garde of the pre-war years. But the early work of Kenneth Anger and Maya Deren made in the mid-1940s was crucially different to most European work, especially in its attempt to deal with the self by using mythical themes and images, and the film-maker as narrative protagonist, as was influentially the case in Deren's *Meshes of the Afternoon* (1943) and Anger's *Fireworks* (1947). Anger's influences are difficult to pin down but he was acquainted with European art cinema and avant-garde work – Eisenstein, Jean Cocteau, D. W. Griffiths and Georges Méliès. He also had met the abstract animator Harry Smith and had seen Deren's *Meshes of the Afternoon*, which he distributed through Creative Film Associates, set up with Curtis Harrington (see Landis 1996: 20–2).

This assumption that the post-war American avant-garde film was simply the child of European modernism (of course Man Ray was American) does not stand up to the evidence. Any screening of Peterson's *Lead Shoes* (1949), Anger's *Fireworks* and Deren's *Meshes of the Afternoon* would reveal a sensibility in all the films which is peculiarly American. P. Adams Sitney has isolated this feeling by identifying an American brand of Romanticism in these post-war works, a strand of creativity which is especially to be found in literature descending from Blake and Wordsworth through the American poets Walt Whitman and Wallace Stevens and finds its critical voice, at least for Sitney, in Harold Bloom's early writings (see Sitney 1979). Lucy Fisher argues that the early American avant-garde cinema 'seems ... fundamentally motivated by an obsession with self-definition' (1976: 69).

Sitney states that 'the recurrent theme of the American avant-garde film is the triumph of the imagination' (1974: 115), thus establishing a way of reading these films within a tradition that is only modernist at the edges, or at least, sees modernism as a moment in a much broader tradition – romanticism. Given the impact of abstract expressionism with its visionary and intensely subjectivist aesthetic in post-war American visual culture, Sitney's interpretation is not a wayward one but in many ways fitting with American visual arts in the 1940s and 1950s. As we shall see, it is with the films of Stan Brakhage that such a view finds most support.

Maya Deren

Deren was thoroughly independent as a film-maker. Her background was not in the visual arts but in literature. Her college thesis had been on the influence of French symbolist poetry on the work of Ezra Pound and T. S. Eliot. She does not have any allegiance to twentieth-century ideas like modernism and surrealism although she mingled freely with the modernist European exile artists gathered in New York during the war and after. Her sympathetic relationship to Marcel Duchamp during this period is understandable especially in her stated allegiance to classicism and arms-length feelings towards both surrealism and romanticism. Duchamp's aesthetic instincts now seem more classical – an objective ordered sensibility albeit not naturalist-realist. It could be argued that there is a shared sensibility between a work like Duchamp's *Etant donnes* (1946–66) and Deren's early films.

Her sense of the aesthetic is a strong one as her writings reveal (Deren 2001). Her work owes more to poetry, dance and mythology than painting or film itself. However, her husband Alexander Hammid, who shot *Meshes of the Afternoon*, was a Czech refugee cameraman and an important avant-garde film-maker in his native Czechoslovakia. He was also familiar with Soviet and British documentary of the pre-war years.

The camerawork of *Meshes* is expressionist in its odd angles as well as in its dreamlike narrative, deriving, as Sitney points out, from a form of somnambulist tradition found in the Romantic tradition but stemming in film terms from Robert Wiene's *The Cabinet of Dr Caligari* (1920). There is no evidence that Deren saw *Caligari* but by then such work was in the air and Hollywood itself was quite capable of an expressionist aesthetic.

Whatever its lineage, *Meshes* stands out for its summation of a tradition in the avant-garde which can be traced through films like Man Ray's *Etoile de mer* (1928), Cocteau's *The Blood of a Poet* (1932) and Germaine Dulac's *Seashell and the Clergyman* (1927), but rendered by Deren with enormous economy and confidence. It pointedly has the charismatic figure of Deren herself at its centre. Its polish and treatment is more reminiscent, it may be argued, of art cinema, however its formal treatment of the theme places it firmly in the avant-garde tradition. *Meshes* concerns the 'interior experiences of an individual' according to Deren (quoted in Sitney 1974) and is not to be associated with the surrealist imagery of Buñuel's *Un Chien Andalou*, although in its structure it echoes Buñuel and Eisenstein's montage.

Meshes has an intricate repeated circular shape, described as spiral by Sitney, which depicts the travails of a woman pursuing a hooded, glass-faced figure. In between, she encounters herself and a man, both objects of her desire but also of her fears and anxiety. Like a dream-state, *Meshes* achieves more continuity (and fiendish complexity) than we would normally associate with a dream (*Un Chien Andalou* comes closer to a dream on that account). For example, at the end of the first section, the protagonist seems to fall asleep in a chair and the film ends with her waking up in the chair, but it is a false ending for she is dead. How far seeing *Meshes* as a dream helps us to understand it is questionable. For Deren it was the expression of a state of mind, which is a different matter from the portrayal of the unconscious, which is only a state of mind when it is remembered. *Meshes* has an intellectual sophistication not usually associated with dreams.

Deren's work was seen by some, especially the Museum of Modern Art curator Iris Barry, as repetitive of the French inter-war avant-garde films of Man Ray and Leger/Murphy (Holl 2001: 162). But Deren's use of montage to establish irrational spaces and times – as in the footsteps sequence in *Meshes* and the similar cutting which is the main formal device of *A Study in Choreography for Camera* (1945) with dancer Talley Beatty – is much more akin to Russian montage techniques. Deren came to realise that it was also owing, albeit unconsciously, to the 'trick' silent Hollywood films, especially Buster Keaton's *Sherlock Junior* (1924), which she had seen as a child.

Deren's early works are an example of what has been called 'psycho-drama' cinema in America in the post-war years. The classics of such an approach include Deren's *Meshes* and *At Land* (1944), Anger's *Fireworks*, Sidney Peterson's *The Lead Shoes* and his *Mr Frenhofer and the Minotaur* (both 1949), Gregory Markopoulous' *Swain* (1950) and Stan Brakhage's early *Desistfilm* (1954). P. Adams Sitney has been the main proponent of the psychodrama as a film genre within the avant-garde, holding that its main characteristic is the 'quest for sexual identity' (1979: 18) and in its pure form the film-maker plays the protagonist, as Anger does in *Fireworks* and Deren does in *Meshes* and *At Land*. Sitney traces one of its forms, the trance film, back to Wiene's *The Cabinet of Dr Caligari* and Cocteau's *The Blood of a Poet* (see Sitney 1979).

A Study in Choreography for Camera

This film depicts a dancer's (Talley Beatty) leap, passing through different locations in filmically constructed space and time. Five of Deren's completed films were concerned with 'dance', fostered by her own interests and involvement with the Katherine Dunham Dance Company in the early 1940s, and later deepened in her studies of Haitian voodoo rituals.

In its format of a film comprising a single sequence – matched by Anger's *Eaux d'artifice* (1953) – it not only turns away from her complex structured mythological works, for example *Meshes of the Afternoon* and *At Land*, but establishes a fascinating genre innovation. Not since the early cinema of Lumière had there been such a simple film, thematically if not formally, as

Figure 4 *A Study in Choreography for Camera* (Maya Deren, 1945)

A Study in Choreography for Camera. Nothing in the European avant-garde prepared the way for its formal purity and rigour. It is also as far removed from the 'other' 1920s avant-garde film movement – the surrealist-cum-dadaist work of Cocteau, Man Ray, Dulac, Clair and Buñuel – as *Meshes of the Afternoon* was close to the same movement. But there is a communality shared by most of her films and that is of dance, of the body choreographed for ritual, and the idea of the body's movement is central to all her work. In *A Study in Choreography for Camera* Deren intended the film 'as a sample of film-dance – that is, a dance so related to camera and cutting that it cannot be "performed" as a unit anywhere but in this particular film' (quoted in Cook 1988: 220).

A Study in Choreography for Camera broke with the narrative-cum-metaphorical projects of her two earlier completed films. Her title reveals her concern for the representational problems of dance being a study for choreography for the *camera* not the dancer. As a 'study' it suggests a genuine experimental work which she perhaps did not intend as a fully-fledged alternative artistic form. It contains formal devices found in the earlier films – repetition structures, spatial and temporal displacements. Deren herself held the view that *A Study in Choreography for Camera* 'was an effort to isolate and celebrate the principle of the power of movement which was contained in *At Land*' (quoted in Sitney 1979: 31).

The film depicts a run, a pirouette and a leap. It begins with a slow pan from right to left of a clearing in a wood. During this almost 360° pan, the dancer appears four times, each time having gone further in his slow spiralling movement from a dancer's crouch, and each time coming closer to the camera. He then extends his foot to place it inside a room. In his run he passes through different locations – rooms, woodlands, a museum courtyard – until the pirouette, during which he passes from a slow-down speed to a very fast one. The film ends with a slow leap, fractured by edits so that time itself is extended as if the dancer were slowly and impossibly soaring through the air. He lands magically back once again in the woodland clearing.

For Sitney, the film has a 'perfection which none of Maya Deren's [other films] achieved' (1979: 25), possibly the result of its more formalist aspiration compared with the two earlier films. For Deren, the dancer's leap is a unified 'primitive' form of expression, in which she allows no elements of filmic or personal indulgence to interfere – it has its own completeness and universality.

Kenneth Anger

Anger made one of his most popular films, *Fireworks,* at the precocious age of 17 in 1947, significantly in Hollywood where he had been raised. He had made several short films before that on the family 16mm Kodak camera. A child of the Hollywood Dream Machine (as a young boy he had a part in Max Rheinhardt's and William Dieterle's *A Midsummer's Night Dream* (1935)), he became both its critic and its celebrant in a film-making career in which only three hours-worth of films have resulted to date.

Anger's classic, *Fireworks*, is a richly inventive poetic work of staggering maturity, both emotionally and stylistically. The hero, played by Anger (suggesting a strong autobiographical feel), undergoes a dreamlike series of sexual and violent experiences. Championed by Cocteau and an inspiration to Jean Genet's *Un Chant d'Amour* (1950), its explicit gay sexuality, visual wit, emotional expressiveness and technical assuredness remain pertinent as an early exploration of sexual identity.

A living myth, Anger's fame would have been guaranteed solely on the basis of his infamous book *Hollywood Babylon*, published originally in France in 1959 and eventually, and only after being 'cleaned up', in America in 1975. In 1949, he began an ambitious feature-length film of which the sumptuous *Puce Moment* (1949) is a fragment released years later. Between 1950 and 1961 Anger lived in Paris, where in 1951 he made *Rabbit's Moon*, which was not released until 1972, only to be replaced by another, shorter, version in 1979. The baroque 'nocturne' *Eaux D'Artifice* of 1953 was only his second completed film. Shot in Tivoli, Italy it remains one of his finest achievements – a highly controlled but ecstatic dream-like film, set to Vivaldi's stirring music.

Returning for a brief period to America in 1954 he made the classic *The Inauguration of the Pleasure Dome* with money bequeathed to him by his recently deceased mother. *The Inauguration of the Pleasure Dome* was the first film in which Anger forged a distinctively elaborate *mise-en-scène* style using ritual, super-imposition, colour and chiaroscuro lighting to evoke 'phantasy' which is essentially subjective-like. Derived from one of Aleister Crowley's dramatic rituals, in which members of a cult masquerade as gods and goddesses, it fully achieves the merging of these ideas with film form. Its rich colour and exotic symbolist costumes, its air of control and artifice, its ornate monumentality and densely associative meanings saturated in mythology provide a unique aesthetic experience whose only rivals are Eisenstein, Cocteau and Michael Powell and Emeric Pressburger.

It was to be the first of a series of more arcane mythological films inspired by the eccentric English occultist Crowley, to whom the film is dedicated. Anger returned to Paris but completed no film work (three major projects – on Cocteau's *Le Jeune Homme et la Mort* (1946), Lautreamont's *Maldoror* (1865) and Pauline Reage's *L'Histoire d'O* – all collapsed).

In 1961 he settled in Brooklyn where trips to Coney Island inspired his next classic, and perhaps most influential, film, *Scorpio Rising* (1963), which successfully employed a modern setting using a bike-boy gang, found footage and a remarkable pop music soundtrack in order to weave an ironic 'blasphemous' critique of modern culture. The film was promptly confiscated by the LAPD. Two years later another fragment of a larger project appeared – *Kustom Kar Kommando*. In 1966 he began shooting *Lucifer Rising*, a much darker, brooding work, but substantial footage was stolen and it was only completed between 1970 and 1980. In the late 1960s and early 1970s he took refuge in London, befriending pop figures like Mick Jagger and Jimmy Page. He cut *Invocation of My Demon Brother* in 1969 using the *Lucifer Rising* footage remaining after the theft.

Eaux D'Artifice

Eaux D'Artifice was shot in the baroque setting of a moonlit garden in Tivoli, Italy. It is a film of captivating mood achieved through its fluid dissolves and chiaroscuro night-blue-tinted moonlight. An eighteenth-century female figure (or so it seems) is seen ever-descending down steep steps past fountains, gargoyles and ornate balustrades, evoking a moment of beauty and vertiginous yearning. The images are perfectly matched to the stirring glissandos of Vivaldi's aching music. A technical and atmospheric masterpiece, it evokes a Paterian epiphanic mood, a moment which would seem to be eternal, as Anger's spiral-like structure returns constantly to the descending figure.

Eaux D'Artifice exemplifies Anger's Eisensteinian sensibility of 'synchronisation of the senses'. Unburdened by narrative, it celebrates the intensity of visual experience and architectural form. It is also a film-poem on cinema as projected light. An internal rhythm is set up between fixed, unmalleable forms – staircases, gargoyles, balustrades – and fluid; trickling, spurting, flowing, streaming, cascading water. The baroque intricacies and virtuousity of the violin are matched by the same qualities of film's own construction. Its avant-gardism is not in its forms, which are all culled from narrative art cinema, but in its celebration of a moment, in its radical dismissal of narrative, its resonance with the *gesamkunstwerk* or total-artwork, artists like Eisenstein and spectacle elements of Hollywood. In its abstracting tendencies – especially its use of cascading water – it is also a descendant of the German abstract avant-garde – at times reminiscent of the pyrotechnics of Fischinger's choreographed abstractions.

Eaux D'Artifice also plays with space. It shifts continually from images representing perspectival space to ones resembling patterns on a flat surface, or, as in some shots, a black void. This effect is seen in the film's opening close-ups of a fountain spurting, the water drops and curves, glistening in the moonlight against the black background. Reflected light pulsates, glows and wet surfaces radiate light. Beauty and the beast. Good and evil. Decadence.

Both Deren and Anger were uninterested in the so-called materialist aspects of film. Neither of them wanted to use film so as to 'distort' images or make them unreadable through intense close-up, loss of focus, fast pans and swivels, end-of-reel flare-outs and so forth. Their cinema is one that holds onto film's intrinsic capacity for the reproduction of reality. Like Eisenstein, they are interested in the creative properties of composition and editing and in Anger's case, colour too. They took pride in the discipline of artistic control, leaving nothing to chance.[1] This brief period of American activity with its emphasis on the individual artist and on a self-expression demanding the film-makers' own presence before the camera, can be seen as a watershed in the history of the avant-garde. For example, Deren's influence is as alive as ever and was to take on a new energy with the emergence of women film-makers as a powerful force in the 1970s.

1 Unlike Brakhage, who pounced on mistakes, accidents and technical distortions as possible subject matter, as part of a creative process which he wanted to display. Brakhage's 'action' films, often made with the gestures associated with abstract expressionist painting, were anathema to Deren and Anger's more 'classical' stance (as it was to Buñuel and others).

6   THE 1950s: THE AESTHETICS OF THE FRAME

After the explosion of activity of the 1940s, primarily on the West Coast, the American film avant-garde's energies subsided during the 1950s, with the bold exception of Stan Brakhage, who established himself as the most important and, as it was to be, the most influential avant-garde film-maker of the post-war period. For supporters and detractors alike he has domi-nated the avant-garde film landscape from the 1950s through to today. The film-makers of the 1940s had dispersed: some moved into the industry, others found their projects frustrated by lack of resources, funds and time, and others left the country – notably Anger and Markopoulous.

Less prolific than Brakhage and very different in his approach, Robert Breer began making films in Paris in the early 1950s. Initially, he set out to follow a painting career and, as we shall see, his more figurative and animation-based aesthetic, with its wit and freewheeling dadaist shapes and strong colours, set up an interesting juxtaposition to Brakhage. But in the early 1950s, living in France, his cultural framework was quite different to Brakhage's. Breer was experimenting in a formalist and quite European painting tradition. He was uninterested in the subjectivist Romantics that Brakhage was grappling with under the influence of the Black Mountain College avant-garde (Sitney 1979). Unlike their predecessors, they were to emphasise the formal qualities of film in securing their own forms of expression. They were to pay close attention, in their different ways, to the discrete potency of the frame, especially Breer as an animator. No longer was the frame simply what captured a reality in front of the camera but rather it became an arena for forms, like the marks made on a canvas. To this extent, their aesthetic was closer to the one being propounded by Greenberg in relation to modernist American painting at the time. Both film-makers came to shed the armory of narratives, myths and bizarre tropes of Surrealism and chose the highly-exposed strategy of finding forms for their own experiences in which the latter remained recognisably subjective.

Stan Brakhage

Influenced in his early years by the trance films of Deren, Anger, Peterson and others, Brakhage came to settle eventually on a form of lyrical film-making which owed as much to his own experiments as it did to modernist poetry of the period emanating from the Black Mountain group. Brakhage had strong associations with the latter, especially through the figures of Charles Olson, Robert Creely and John Cage, as well as the abstract expressionist painters who found their only truly filmic counterpart in Brakhage (Sitney 1974; Wees 1992). To this extent Brakhage can be seen in retrospect to be the film-maker who shared in the forging of an American visual art style through the impact of European modernism on post-war America.

The antipathy to abstract graphic cinema of Deren and many of the political documentary figures of American independent cinema is not shared by Brakhage, who embraced abstraction as well as the film as material in a way which was anathema to Deren and others. Thus, Brakhage is the first truly modernist American film-maker in terms of the movement's 'return to materials' war cry. His notion of the artist is at the same time deeply Romantic and essentially nature-based, as opposed to Deren's essentially urban stance in the European-influenced New York bohemia, which she occupied until she died. Brakhage's relationship to nature is intrinsic to much major American art, from its early days right through to the land art work of Robert Smithson and Walter de Maria. It is a tradition dominated by a visionary and mythological quality touched by a traditional notion of the sublime. Like the other American modernists, Brakhage, especially in the larger projects like *The Art of Vision* (1961–65) and *Songs* (1964–69), marries an essentially American Romanticism of personal struggle against nature with a modernist self-reflexivity.

Brakhage places himself firmly in a Romanticist aesthetic buried at the heart of certain forms of modernism. The way to modernism was paved by intense subjectivism, a search for certainties outside traditional conventions which had become objectified in rigid 'universal' ideas about both the role of art and its forms. The idea of personal expression, imagination and communication is what disrupted this universalism and it is the legacy of the original Romantic movement of the late eighteenth and early nineteenth century to art in the twentieth century.

Against Deren's dislike of 'personal' film-making, which she associated with the uncontrolled subjectivity of surrealism and expressionism, Brakhage's art is a celebration of an intense subjectivity in which the camera became an intuitive instrument of expression of the body and eye. Central to his aesthetic is the idea of the 'untutored eye' by which he meant a kind of innocence in relation to nature and the world, allowing a return to a vision untrammeled by ideological, cultural, even conceptual baggage (see James 1989: 36–49; Keller 1986: 179–229). Of course, Brakhage's aesthetic was not one of a desultory shooting of whatever fell before the camera. In fact his work on the film was often such as to physically debilitate him. Nevertheless the accidental, the intuitive and spontaneous played an enormous role in his practice and film-making process.

Brakhage has been a prolific film-maker, constantly developing and exploring film forms and materials. His work is largely in 16mm (there is also a body of successful Standard 8 films and more recently painting directly onto 35mm and IMAX formats). The lineage goes through early film-makers like Lye who painted directly onto film. But Brakhage's abstract experiments are not to be aligned with the more controlled graphic tradition of Lye, Richter, Ruttmann *et al.* but rather with the more mercurial, spontaneous brush-mark work of the post-war American abstract expressionist painters and Marie Menken's early diary films, in which colour, shape and movement are used to depict ordinary objects and events. Brakhage's departure from the psychodrama form is marked by *Anticipation of the Night* (1958), at which time he stated in his influential text *Metaphors on Vision* that he 'grew very quickly as a film artist once I got rid of drama as prime source of inspiration' (quoted in Sitney 1979: 147).

Anticipation of the Night

Anticipation of the Night (1958) has been seen as Brakhage's moment of self-discovery and at the same time the founding of his own aesthetic (James 1989: 41–2).[1] The sense of a new beginning was further supported by Brakhage embarking on the writing of his book *Metaphors on Vision*. *Anticipation of the Night* marks his break with any idea of film drama, and according to Sitney it heralds the forming of *lyric* film. For him, the film's 'greatest achievement ... is the distillation of an intense and complex interior crisis into an orchestration of sights and associations which cohere in a new formal rhetoric of camera movement and montage' (1974: 143–4).

Influenced by some of the brief film poems of Marie Menken, Brakhage established a film form which had never been seen before. By contrast, Anger's and Deren's film and many of the post-war West Coast film-makers had explored a form of dramatics, in which the film-maker sometimes was the protagonist. The influence was less modernist, more a symbolist one. With *Anticipation of the Night* Brakhage showed the extent to which he had absorbed influences as varied as the Black Mountain poets, abstract expressionist painting and of course the Romantic movement, sieved through an American modernist sensibility which embraced the poets Olsen, Creely, Pound and avant-garde writer Gertrude Stein (James 1989: 39–41). There is a spontaneity, a hand-held 'action'-feel to the film's images and construction. The movement and editing suggests a direct response of the artist to the world and an expression of his emotional response to it.

In *Anticipation of the Night* Brakhage's style and methodology is imaginatively set out in its editing patterns (fast dense repetitions), rapid camera rhythms, use of focus and aperture to allow detail and light as expressive means and in its intense sense of the camera as forging the style and not simply capturing a compositional 'look'. While a strong trace of the trance film of his previous years remains in the final images of the young man's (played by Brakhage) suicide, Brakhage is attempting primarily to capture the 'innocent' eye of Wordsworthian childhood (and even earlier).

The film's overall impression is of darkness, now and then penetrated by light and colour. In its abstractionist sensibility it reaches back to Man Ray, Leger and of course Menken. The night scenes of fairground lights are reminiscent of the night lights of Ray's *Return to Reason*. And in its shifting repetitions, it has its precursor in Leger's *Ballet Mecanique,* but its intrinsic lyricism and expressiveness stems mainly from Menken's delicate film poems with their spontaneous, tremulous feel, far removed from the more rigid framing of the pre-war makers.

It is in *Anticipation of the Night* that we can appreciate the complex levels of movements possible in film – movement of the camera, movement of rapid editing and of repetitions, and of course the movement within the frame which is the result of the camera movement itself. It is one of the in-built perceptual assumptions we have that we can discern movement in the frame as being just that – stemming from the movements of objects in the real world and the movement of the latter brought about by the movement of the camera. Brakhage has often cultivated in his films this distinction between *what seems to be the case* and *what is the case* and the ambiguity between these two conditions. At times in *Anticipation of the Night* it is as if the world is careering past the static camera as opposed to what we know is the opposite case.

For Sitney the lyrical film of which *Anticipation of the Night* is a supreme example 'postulates the film-maker behind the camera as the first-person protagonist of the film ... the images of the film are what he sees, filmed in such a way that we never forget his presence and we know how he is reacting to his vision' (1979: 142). Of course this is, at one level, a stylistic device. Brakhage in the strict sense is no more or less the active film-maker than any other avant-garde or art film-maker. Just as the distinctiveness of the brushmarks signals the presence of the painter, so to speak, more than does the glazed polished classical style, nevertheless in both cases the painter painted what we see. It is simply that one styles *suggests* that authorship more than the other.

But, importantly, it is also an *expressive* device in that it suggests a different relationship in the case of painting between the artist, the brush (or whatever marking instrument including the artist's own hands and fingers) and the marks on the surface. For Brakhage, the painting model is important, for he is attempting to establish a similar relationship between the artist, the camera and the filmic image. In no other art movement was such a relationship so central as in American abstract expressionism to which Brakhage subscribed. The relationship between artist and brush/camera was one that embraced spontaneity, accident and the action of the body itself.

As we have noted, *Anticipation of the Night* is an early successful and ambitious example of Brakhage's lyrical aesthetic which he had been developing in such films as *Whiteye* and *Loving* (both 1957). For Sitney, *Anticipation of the Night* is about suicide and its context, thus it is to be associated with the psychodramas of Anger and Deren. But unlike the latter it does not create through film a fictional/mythical narrative or *mise-en-scène* for such an action but seems to be of a more universal nature – a man and a series of images of a general kind – children on a merry-go-round, night skies, undergrowth, a baby on a lawn, trees, the moon and sun and so forth. There is no fully-fledged psychodramatic story or drama. In fact the only temporal connection is between the early shots of a man's shadow walking in a doorway and the shadow of his hanging body. What occurs in between has no real temporal structure at all. It could be a collection of memories or images organised around non-temporal means. Of course, it has a time structure in film terms, but no temporal causation between items. Wees describes the film as symbolic especially in its hanged man. For Brakhage, the film is metaphorical: 'all of childhood was just an anticipation of the night of adulthood' (quoted in Wees 1992: 90). He was to reject metaphor soon after this film as he moved towards a 'visionary' cinema which did not rely on any dramatic, mythological or symbolic underpinnings.

Robert Breer

Robert Breer's paintings were in the hard-edged abstraction mode of the neo-plasticians. Originally influenced by Mondrian and Kandinsky, who were fashionable in the post-war French art world, Breer turned to film in the early 1950s. He used the same aesthetic, reminiscent of Richter's experiments in the 1920s, even though he was barely aware of the German graphic avant-garde's work (Sitney 1979: 275–82). His early work emanates from the strong version of abstraction discussed in Chapter 2.

Breer made a series of films when he began experimenting with the moving image, which included *Form Phases IV* (1954), a formal working of largely basic geometric shapes in space using colour. Breer's reference points and framework are decidedly non-literary and non-dramatic. Unlike Brakhage, contemporary abstract painting is the starting point of Breer's artistic problems devolving into film. In these early years, Breer is firmly in the absolute cinema tradition of the German graphic animation movement of Richter, Ruttmann and Fischinger. It is only later in his career that Breer begins to acknowledge the Hollywood cartoon tradition which in itself was essentially a graphic visual system and not a literary one (see Klein 1993).

However, the free-flowing fast collage-montage *Recreation* (1956–7) owed more to the Dada tradition of Man Ray and Leger than to the graphic animation of the German avant-garde. Moving back to America, Breer seemed much more at home with the burgeoning Pop art scene and the fluxus 'happenings' of the 1960s, encouraging a more culturally sensitive and ultimately more personal approach in his work which began to deal with the banalities, joys and miseries of domestic life. A self-deprecating humour and, at times, pathos not commonly found in the avant-garde tradition since the early 1920s dominated his work.

There are similarities with Brakhage. Breer would also at a certain important point turn his cinema into a partially documentary one using his family and domestic surroundings as a source of inspiration and subject matter. Though for Breer, these domestic film scenarios are less intrusive and less raw, being mediated through drawings and the film-maker's fundamental humour and wit, plus a humane and again touching self-deprecation which is missing from Brakhage's work.

A Man and His Dog Out for Air

In *Form Phases IV* (1954) there is a brief sequence in which hand-drawn curving lines change shape. It can be seen as a precursor of his classic *A Man and His Dog Out for Air* (1957) made a few years later. The latter comprises black-line drawing on a white background. This simple format allows him enormous freedom to transform the screen into different spatial types. At times it is simply lines on a flat surface, but, at others, as a line suggests a bird or a horizon or hill, the surface is momentarily transformed into three-dimensional space, but only briefly as continually shifting lines evolve into something abstract denying the space just constructed. In this way, *A Man and His Dog Out for Air* is reminiscent of a more anarchic free-flowing Fischinger-like aesthetic in which formal shapes become figurative ones – flowers, birds, waves and so on. Shifts from two- to three-dimensional space are continual and momentary, teasing the viewer.

The other major element in the film is Breer's use of live-action sounds – in this case a bird loudly twittering establishing an accompanying aural space. The traditional use of music as accompaniment to abstract graphic films – for example in the work of Len Lye, Harry Smith, Oskar Fischinger – which had typically reinforced the abstract/generalised nature of such work, is opened up by Breer to a realist-cum-naturalist representational form. Breer was to explore this live-sound/animated-image relationship more thoroughly in the films of the 1960s and afterwards (especially *69* [1968] and *LMNO* [1978]). An upshot of this is that the internal rhythms of the film are not distorted or assisted by musical rhythms as in so much animation. Instead Breer favours noises – taps running, dogs yapping, dishes clattering, aeroplanes passing overhead and where music occurs, it is more like someone practising on the piano at home.

In this more personal expressive approach, Breer was not so far removed from Brakhage's work, although their forms, themes and passions were of quite different orders. But both of them signifed a definite break with

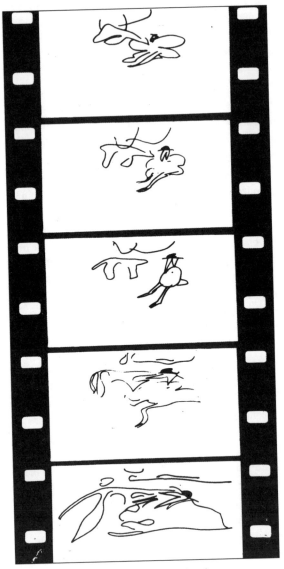

Figure 5   *A Man and His Dog Out For Air* (1957)

the classical rigour, and objectivity almost, of Deren and Anger's films. Brakhage and Breer are committed modernists in their use of spontaneous expression, self-reflexivity and sensitivity to film's materiality.

Part of this expressivity, shared with Brakhage, lies in Breer's commitment to drawing. Although using traditional roto-scoping (tracing frame-by-frame over live-action footage) to achieve natural movement, there is a chaotic aspect to the drawings that is definitely hand-made. In *A Man and His Dog Out for Air* the free-hand drawings have a vibrancy from its 'boiling' (the wriggling outlines caused by imperfect registration) and caricatural style.

Breer can be seen as someone who revives the true graphic tradition of the American cartoon, lost in the early 1930s. In more recent years he has acknowledged his cartoon precursors, especially Otto Messmer's Felix the Cat. Norman Klein argues that 'while [the pre-1934 cartoon] makes allusion to story, its primary responsibility is to surface, rhythm, and line' (1993: 5). The same could be said of Breer's films.

Breer's embracing of a popular art form alongside his roots in high-art German avant-garde abstractionism, is at one with a general turning of the American film avant-garde in the late 1950s and 1960s to popular culture for its images, sensibilities and energy as found in the films of Bruce Conner, Jack Smith, Andy Warhol, Kenneth Anger and Joseph Cornell. *A Man and His Dog Out for Air* is an early version of such a merging with its finally constructed image from the abstract lines of a child-like cartoon man and his dog strolling off the screen.

While the 1950s is usually seen as a quiet period in the American avant-garde dominated by the fairly isolated Brakhage, towards the end of the decade new ideas and approaches began to emerge. On the West Coast Bruce Conner, a 'junk' sculptor, made *A Movie* in 1957, although his work only began to appear in the 1960s. Harry Smith, Stan Vanderbeek, the Whitney Brothers, Willard Maas and Marie Mencken were also working, though often fitfully during the 1950s. The other major impetus was around the Beat generation (see James 1989; Wolf 1997) with Ken Jacob's *Star Spangled to Death* appearing in 1957, although he was to be most prolific in the avant-garde explosion of the 1960s, with classics like *Little Stabs at*

Happiness and *Blonde Cobra* (both 1959–63) surfacing in the early 1960s although begun in the late 1950s.

In the work of Brakhage and Breer, strong modernist values are established in the film avant-garde. For the first time formalist exploration and innovation is in the service of an intensely personal cinema. Any pretensions to a neo-Platonist objectivism are thrown aside and an intensity of expression is achieved that, it could be argued, was only truly matched by Len Lye in the pre-war period. Both film-makers aligned themselves with the broader American avant-garde, Brakhage with the poets of the Black Mountain college and Breer, in the early 1960s, with Kinetic art and 'happenings'.

1   The best writing on this film remains Sitney's in *Visionary Film* (1979). On Brakhage see James's sympathetic but critical viewpoint in *Allegories of Cinema* (1989).

7   THE 1960s: THE NEW WAVE

The inclusion of a chapter on the New Wave in a book dedicated to avant-garde film may raise eyebrows in some quarters. For some, the flourishing New Wave films of the 1960s are not deemed avant-garde at all but on the contrary, 'derive from the commercial, narrative cinema' (Le Grice 1976: 100; see also Gidal 1989: 26). The most influential New Wave was a group of films made in France in the late 1950s and early 1960s, namely Claude Chabrol's *Le Beau Serge* (1958) and especially François Truffaut's *Le Quarte cents coups* (1959) which attracted much media attention. These two films were followed by Eric Rohmer's *Le signe du lion* (1959), Jacques Rivette's *Paris nous appartient* (1960) and, famously, Godard's *A bout de souffle* (1959). But there were 'New Waves' in other countries too – notably Germany, Yugoslavia, Czechoslovakia and Italy.

For the 'traditional' avant-garde, the New Wave made too many con-cessions to mainstream cinema – their narratives, their formal conserva-tism, their relatively large budgets, their use of professional actors and 'stars' and their place in the 'art cinema' exhibition circuit. There is more agreement about their identity as modernists, which does not necessarily imply their being in the advanced guard of cinema but rather sharing a certain sensibility and set of attitudes to film and the world in general. In some ways they can be seen as similar to the first French avant-garde of Epstein *et al.* They share the latter's experimental approach to narrative, *mise-en-scène* and psychological expressionism. In other words it is a form of experimental art cinema which remains committed to a broader audience.

The inclusion of certain film-makers of the European New Waves also owes much to their impact on women film-makers who demanded a return to a more narrative-based cinema but one that used radical forms and lastly, and importantly, engaged with cultural and political issues and themes. In America, Yvonne Rainer began to evolve such a cinema derived from Godard. In Britain, his influence has perhaps been more marked. From the works of Laura Mulvey and Peter Wollen in the 1970s (see Mulvey 1989: 49–62) to the work of the New Romantics John Maybury, Cerith Wyn Evans and the black cinema of Isaac Julien and others, Godard's political stance, collaging techniques and his use of an essayist form (with visual footnotes) has been a consistent reference point (O'Pray 2001).

The French and Italian New Waves were to have an impact on the American 'movie brats' – Francis Ford Coppola, George Lucas, Steven Spielberg, Martin Scorsese and William Friedkin – who emerged in the 1970s. The latter's sensibilities, ambitions and cultural-cum-political reference-points were informed by the European movement to such an extent that it acted as an avant-garde for the American mainstream. At the same time, Godard and Jean-Marie Straub/Daniele Huillet were being lauded by the New Left for their political modernism. Godard was exemplary of what Peter Wollen (1982) called 'counter-cinema'. He is also a prime member of one wing of Wollen's 'two avant-gardes'. The latter understanding of film avant-gardism has been one of the most influential in academic circles over the past two decades. It is both a historical distinction and a formal one. It responds not only to a tension but an antagonism at times between two broad historical streams of radical film-making. Counter-cinema, according to Wollen, was characterised by particular points of transgression of mainstream Hollywood rules. While this cinema was not anti-narrative, it did however reveal its means of narrativising. It allowed the construction of narrative to be part of its form and thus was self-reflexive, modernist in its aims. It was also a cinema that was seen to mount a substantial critique of mainstream cinema.

Appropriately, Wollen and film theorist Mulvey committed themselves to a 'political' avant-garde cinema in Britain in the 1970s with their film *Riddles of the Sphinx* (1977), in which similar strategies were used to critique the mainstream's codes and conventions, undermining its ideological presuppositions and freeing film for more critical, if not revolutionary purposes. Mulvey's 1975 seminal essay on visual pleasure was the beginnings of a theoretical founding for such a cinema (especially for the burgeoning women's cinema), one which would eschew 'visual pleasure' for the more Godardian and Brechtian 'pains' of Marxist and Freudian knowledge.

Jean-Luc Godard

Shot in black and white and structured in 12 episodes, Godard's early film *Vivre sa vie* (1962) has an aspiring actress-cum-prostitute, Nana, as its central character, played by Anna Karina, Godard's wife at the time. The film points forward to *Two or Three Things I Know About Her* (1966) in its documentary-like analysis of prostitution sieved through French laws and the pimp's rules (in voice-over), undercut by the formal montage of Nana plying her trade. The film, like *Bande à part* (1964), *Masculin Feminin* (1966), is another portrait of Karina, who flips from coquette to depressive, with a dance sequence round the pool table, a precursor of her dance in *Bande à part* and in *Pierrot le fou* (1965) with Jean-Paul Belmondo. It is also a film which pays homage to Rossellini's *Rome Open City* (1945) in its final sequence depicting the casual shooting of Nana, rhyming Anna Magnani's similar death in the Italian Neo-realist classic. In many ways *Vivre sa vie* has been seen by commentators as much less radical or 'avant-garde' than the work of the Dziga-Vertov group period, especially *Vent D'est* (1970) or *Weekend* (1967) or, for that matter, *Two or Three Things I Know About Her*.

The attempts by film-makers to separate themselves from a monolithic mainstream have been guided by two lights – a critical relationship to it and on the other hand an association by some to the fine art modernism tradition with its own avant-gardes especially in painting and sculpture (and to some extent in literature, music, dance, theatre and performance). The former reaction has been related by Wollen to a political critique in which form serves political ends, and in the latter to a more formalist critique which questions what he sees as the ontological status of film itself – what kind of thing is cinema/film? (1982b). Of course this is a question also asked by Eisenstein, but without the formal avant-garde's scepticism as to the possibility of an image or of events imaged in space and time. For Godard, film is a medium already defined by narrative and not simply the sum of its *material* processes, and the question, for him, is never one of a return-to-zero in the way it was for some of the 'co-op' avant-gardists in the 1960s.

But Godard's films before 1968 are also personal ones. They are passionate essays on the world and on film-making, refusing the solace of narrative. Godard saw himself more as a journalist than as a novelist, perpetrating sealed-off stories which he associated with mainstream films. Gilberto Perez comments that a 'Godard film gives the impression not of the complete but of the ongoing, a world in process of taking place' (1998: 337).

Two or Three Things I Know About Her

Two or Three Things is a kaleidoscope of filmic approaches and strategies. It is in part a document of Paris – its cafés, streets, but especially building sites and new motorway bypasses; it is also part-fictional but uses at times a documentary-style to explore women's ennui, their mental states – indifference and alienation. Furthermore, it is an excuse for asking questions of a philosophical, sociological and aesthetic nature (problems in a sceptical vein of film style and expression), sometimes through Godard's own whispering, insinuating voice-over, and sometimes through the mouths of his housewives, saleswomen and part-time prostitutes.

The Third World, American imperialism in Vietnam (ongoing at the time) and burgeoning working-class consumerism form a backdrop. It is also a film of controlled colour – primarily white, blue, red and orange. If this is a film with a political address, it is also one of subjective feelings, doubts and thoughts. It has also been characterised as 'icy poetry' (see Monaco 1976: 153–86) in which Rimbaud and Cocteau are twin influences.

Interestingly, at a time when structuralism as a methodology was dominating French culture, Godard's philosophical questions are mainly Sartrean – they deal primarily with a personal anguish and with the gap between 'the objectivity that crushes me ... the subjectivity that isolates me' (Godard in *Two or Three Things*). It is also the case that the seats of consciousness, of critique, of melancholic estrangement in the film are women. Men are mechanics, pimps and johns with very little to say of interest. In key sequences male characters repeat or regurgitate what others have said or written, acting like vociferous consumers of the word – written and spoken. Women on the other hand pose questions of self-identity, of meaning and existential anxiety. Gender seems to separate different concerns in the world – for men, an obsession with machines, politics (but not political action) and sex; for women, fashion, shopping, children and alienation.

But the overriding voice is that of Godard himself. On the soundtrack he whispers his questions, his conundrums, his analyses, his reflections on objects, life, politics, philosophy and on his own images, his own attempts to wrestle meaning from the world through the medium of film. In the final moments of the film, Juliette – housewife and part-time prostitute – reads in bed with her husband, engaging in a desultory conversation with him about trivia and about her life: 'I've changed and I'm still the same.' As throughout the film, the colours are strong primary ones: the husband's blue shirt, the bed's red blanket and the green of the painting hanging above it. She lights a cigarette and the film cuts to an intense close-up of the flame and glowing cigarette end – like a planet engulfed with fire or the microscopic stuff of matter itself. The whispering voice-over (Godard's, not Juliette's) tells how on listening to an Esso ad on the transistor radio (at the time, hi-tech) 'I drive off without a care on the road to dreams. I forget Hiroshima, Auschwitz, Budapest. [The image changes to the word 'Idées'.] I forget Vietnam, the housing problems, the famine in India. [Cut to a shot, slowly pulling back, of various packaged products set out on grass like a small city.] I forget everything except that I'm back at zero ... and have to start from there'. The image darkens. Four chords of music. And then the film ends.

It is the shifting levels of images – naturalism in the bedroom, almost abstract close-up of the cigarette, text, the theatrical layout of consumer products and then darkness – that would offer means of exploring political issues as they revolve around the personal. The sound also shifts – the casual chat of a couple in bed, the whispering voice (of whom?) placed outside the film text, and the fragment of music. How the voice and thoughts of Juliette are transferred to a man, to the all-controlling voice of the director. Despite problems felt by feminists in Godard's ambivalence towards his women characters, there are structures here that open up possibilities for film-making that desires the ability to amalgamate the personal, the symbolic, the abstract and so forth.

Michelangelo Antonioni

If an important response to traditional film by Godard was his knowing caricature and later documentary-real, Michelangelo Antonioni, in the 1960s, by contrast, remains loyal to the narrative, to the fictional character, to film as an expressive whole. For example, the world of the three Monica Vitti films (*L'avventura* [1960], *L'eclisse* [1962], *Il deserto rosso* [1964]) is far from that of Godard's films of the same period. The continual hustle and bustle, exits and entries, montage-clutter, staccato-philosophising of Godard is set against Antonioni's measured sense of space, quiet, stasis and genuine cool contemplation. Unlike Antonioni, Godard's *belle-lettres*, essayist mentality has never sustained narrative in any responsible way.

But what is avant-garde about Antonioni? Recognised as a supreme master of the art cinema he would seem to be discounted on the grounds of the narrative coherence and low-key innovation of his 1960s films. But this is to be too easily seduced by comparison with Godard's recurring return-to-zero strategies. Antonioni's contribution flies to the heart of film as a medium, largely through his ability to open up new forms of expression through his use of time, space and narrative. It is perhaps no accident that he is often preferred to Godard by some co-op avant-gardists. This is perhaps to do with a more poetic approach to the medium and a more sustained exploration of the long-take plus an exemplary taste for visual ambiguity.

Antonioni had established a serious reputation throughout the 1950s with *Le amiche* (1955) and *Il grido* (1957), but it was *L'avventura* which established his international reputation as a leading figure of the New Wave. *L'avventura* was an enormous international success after being booed at the Cannes Film Festival. Its modernism lies in its textual openness, lack of narrative closure, its anti-narrative structure and ambiguity, spatial awareness and resistance to fixed meanings. It also deals with contemporary bourgeois life in a way that was still fairly uncommon at the time. Compared with Godard, Antonioni's films embrace narrative, never allowing self-referential devices to puncture its representation. For example, actors never look into the camera or address the audience.

L'avventura's locations are a mix of traditional and modern, with a sense of deserted spaces and places often at the fringes of towns (cf. Fellini), depicting a deep sense of displacement, alienation and existential anxiety. Its subject-matter – the search for a missing woman – is typically left unresolved. In many ways Antonioni is a realist who understands the complexity of such a position in art. Filmically literal, he shows only what is there, but through ellipses and use of dead-time – thus developing Rossellini's work and the shot composition of figures in space, he implies a level of presence/absence that has been difficult for critics/theorists to articulate.

L'eclisse

Made in 1961 directly after *La Notte* (1961), *L'eclisse* is the most experimental of these films of the early 1960s. Set in Rome it depicts a brief affair between Vittoria (Vitti), a translator, and Piero (Alain Delon), a stock exchange jobber. Sitney argues that Antonioni's films reflect the 'boom' years of the Italian economy; it is set in the EUR district, 'a display zone of contemporary architecture and city planning' (1995: 159) of fascist origin which became a show piece for the Italian 'economic miracle'.

Figure 6   *L'eclisse* (Michelangelo Antonioni, 1961)

L'eclisse was embraced by 1960s Italians in terms of the ideas of Marxism, psychoanalysis and philosophy (see Sitney 1995: 155–60). For some, it is a film about the re-ordering of our experience of the contemporary world (Rohdie 1990; Perez 1998: 367–416). It has also been understood as a film primarily exploring film form (Brunette 1998).

The film depicts a strong difference and attraction between a young energetic stockbroker obsessed by money and material things and a thoughtful intellectual concerned with knowledge and memory. Architecture and a modernist sense of space dominates the film – from the fragmented apartment of her ex-lover to the expansive echoing chamber of the Milan stock exchange where monetary rationalism meets an intuitive superstition (Vitti's mother) and Vitti's repulsed fascination but, finally, scepticism.

Like Fellini (oddly) *L'eclisse* has consciousness as its subject-matter – not by way of Felliniesque-fantasy, but rather of the perception and knowledge of Vitti's organising point of view. However, the film's modernism traces not only the disconnectedness of things/events but also the struggle to reconstitute (through consciousness) what is precarious and always dissolving. It is also a film which expresses Antonioni's viewpoint, often creating a strange, dream-like quality.

For example, at the end of their long walk together after their witnessing of the car's retrieval from the dock, Vittoria and Piero approach a street corner. In a head and shoulders two-shot, he says to her 'When we get there, I'm going to kiss you.' She looks disturbed. They walk out of shot. There is a cut to a high, moving shot above them as they walk disconnected across the zebra crossing, during which he glances at her. They stop half-way and turn to the right. There is a cut to a head two-shot. She says 'We're half way.' They move again, the camera with them; he is looking at her, she is looking ahead. They move off shot right. Cut to the corner momentarily empty, then with them entering the frame from the left. Vittoria stops, the back of head to camera, and he walks around her to right of frame, so that we see his face. He moves to the fence and she follows at a distance, the camera having moved to the right to encompass both of them. He turns and rests against the fence, she crosses the screen to the left of him. Cut to a shot of tree branches moving in the wind. Cut to side view of a couple with Piero near camera looking out of screen right, Vittoria behind him facing the fence; she turns her head to look at him and smiles. He notices and moves towards her placing his back to the camera and hiding her. The camera moves to the other side in head-shot as Piero kisses her at which there is a cut to the previous camera position, Piero's back to the camera. We see her flinch from and avoid the kiss. Cut back to a shot of the back of Vittoria's head and Piero's face; he moves back and she crosses past him, as the camera moves back. He is once more on the right of shot, resting back on the fence; she is on the left of shot, at the end of the fence. She remarks 'I'm leaving'. Close-up of a water barrel, into which she drops a peg? Cut back as she leaves to right and he follows her into the road. Cut to a moving shot of her walking back to camera. She stops and turns. Cut to shot behind her looking back at the corner from where he has disappeared. She turns and walks out of shot left. The shot of the empty space is held for a few seconds.

This complex sequence exemplifies Antonioni's use of figures (Vittoria and Piero), objects (the road, water barrel, fence, trees and so forth) and events (walking, looks, a kiss [evaded], utterings) in screen-space to express complex feelings (see Perez 1998: 383–4). A sense of estrangement operates not only between characters, but also between them and their own desires, and more fundamentally, between them and the world itself. It is a crucial scene in the characters' relationship. Piero's promised (threatened?) kiss disrupts everything. Its enacting depends on the couple reaching a physical point in space – 'there' – and from that moment in the sequence, Antonioni renders space and its contents as intensely 'present'. For example, the moving high-angle shot of their walk across the zebra crossing expresses a series of elements – the tension of a promised and potential intimacy (the kiss) between them, and the distance that intimacy has to cross to be fulfilled. There is also the distance of directorial regard.

Parallel to the modernist reflexive concern in *L'eclisse* is a more political one, a critique of the Italian 1960s economic 'boom' and its attendant materialism, and even of capitalism. But there is also a nod towards broader issues, especially that of nuclear threat, in *L'eclisse*'s famous final montage sequence. The film is rich at many levels – psychological, political, phenomenological – and has divided critics between a modernist open-textured interpretation and a more existentialist one about our alienated place in modern society.

Red Desert (1964) is the last film of the Vitti series. This time Vitti plays the mentally disturbed wife of an industrialist whose young son seems to have a paralytic (psychosomatic?) illness from which he recovers. She has a relationship with Corrado, a visiting engineer/factory owner. The narrative is from the wife's point of view, in a more substantial way than any of his previous films. Pier Paolo Pasolini argued at the time that Antonioni 'no longer hangs his vision of the world … on a vaguely sociological content (the neurosis of alienation): rather he looks at the world through the eyes of a sick woman … he has identified his own delirious vision with the vision of a neurotic' (quoted in Sitney 1995: 210).

Red Desert was Antonioni's first film in colour, which he uses in an expressive and highly manipulative way. As the film is set in the polluted landscape of the oil industries around Ravenna (Po delta), the distinctive 'sickly' coloration also expresses the wife's state of mind. The film uses pollution as a metaphor (an infernal landscape) for the wife's mental state (or perhaps it is a genuine cause or part-cause of her 'neurosis' – typically the film is ambiguous). It has also been argued that there is an ambiguity as to whether the film's colours and aesthetic strategies represent the wife's feelings or Antonioni's (see Pasolini above for one interpretation). Antonioni deploys a non-realist use of colour – at times literally painting trees and so forth – except for the storytelling sequence, thus reversing the normal colour codes. Using a short focus lens Antonioni often deploys out-of-focus effects to render near-abstraction (reminiscent of Rothko whom he had met and admired). It is also a story of sexual repression and awakening of the Vitti character, especially in light of the story she tells her son and her sexual refusal of her husband and Corrado for much of the film.

Antonioni's modernism in the film is akin to that associated with the abstract expressionist school, with its emphasis on expression, unconscious motivation, anti-naturalist and abstractionist tendencies, together with his camerawork and graphic compositional formalism. As Pasolini suggests, it is one of the most aestheticised of his films, moving strongly towards a poetics of vision which Pasolini himself was to embrace. The notion of alienation is weaker because of the implied mental state of the central character, nevertheless there is strong support for a view of Italian culture being unrooted, mechanistic (and male) and brutally indifferent to anything much outside capitalism and the cynically held conventions of the social (marriage, for example).

Daniele Huillet and Jean-Marie Straub

If Godard was largely an 'avant-garde' chronicler of contemporary France in the 1960s, and Antonioni of the alienated Italian bourgeoisie, then Jean-Marie Straub and Daniele Huillet were more closely identified with formally 'pure' but historical literary-based projects in their three major works of the 1960s, *Not Reconciled* (1964–65), *Chronicle of Anna Magdalena Bach* (1967) and *The Bridegroom, the Actress and the Pimp* (1968), even though the latter had a contemporary setting. All these film-makers shared a form of political modernism characteristic of European avant-garde film-making in the 1960s and 1970s, therefore notions of 'modernism' and 'avant-garde' are often interchangeable in writing about these film-makers.[1]

Straub and Huillet's work has been aligned with Brecht's critique of traditional theatre forms, with the accent on anti-psychologism and anti-Aristotelean catharsis, and establishing a pedagogical approach in which a Marxist class analysis dominates (see Bloch *et al.* 1977). The former characteristics are more easily recognisable in these films than a full-blown Marxist analysis. However, there is a 'materialist' approach to film in which the means of representation, so to speak, are pushed into the foreground in any experience of the film. As Richard Roud states of their films 'they are concerned with the processes and materials of film itself' (1972: 11). This is something they share with Godard's mid-to-late 1960s work as discussed above. But there is also a more precise formal unity to a film like *Chronicle of Ann Magdalena Bach* as compared with the freewheeling multi-textual collage impulse of Godard's *Two or Three Things I Know About Her.*

Chronicle of Anna Magdalena Bach

Filmic space was central to Straub and Huillet's aesthetic. They favoured the static long-take diagonal shot which in *Chronicle* is underpinned by their desire to preserve the integrity of the musical performances in the film. If Godard prefers more frontal shots and tracking, and Antonioni a more disruptive space, then Straub and Huillet cut through space in a more dramatic way by the diagonal shot, accentuating a perspectivally organised space. These blocks of time and space are counterpointed to the pans and tilts and flurries of editing which reflect respectively Bach's choral blocks and rhythms. The most obvious point to make about the diagonal shot is that it is unique to cinema unlike the theatrical 'frontal' shot.

As with their major influence Robert Bresson, *Chronicle* is acted in a expressionless way, a deadpan acting-out of even the most dramatic and emotional scenes in Magdalena Bach's fictionalised 'document'. This is also the case in Godard's *Two or Three Things* except there the emphasis is often on placing emotional or philosophical dialogue in the mouths of the most mundane and unlikely characters, emphasising the disjunction between certain kinds of discourse and their perpetrators – an ironic and satiric strategy. *Chronicle* does not undermine the narrative's seriousness or emotional states but rather refuses psychologistic characterisation as the main means of expressing it.

In *Chronicle* Straub and Huillet have made a deceptively complex film in which different elements – Bach's music, its performance, historical documents, architectural features, fictional voice-over and the film itself – are to some degree autonomous and yet intricately woven. Subtle differences of *mise-en-scène* are set up to suggest a more emotional expressiveness, running counter to its surface formalism. For example, most of the musical performances take place in ornate baroque interiors, the musicians and singers bewigged and frock-coated. Long, deep diagonal shots, often cramping the performers in the space, are typically used to such an extent that Bach himself is reduced to a figure in the background, barely discernible from the other musicians. Over the film's duration, this has the cumulative effect of expressing the composer's often cramped and restrictive working conditions, financial straits and lack of recognition. Thus, while the film elaborates Bach's more mundane and material context, the film's framing and editing evokes an emotional response to him.

In comparison, when Anna Magdelena is shown playing alone at home, the domestic interiors are plain and simple, and her music suggests a private interiority and meditative quality denied by the pompous baroque interiors of her husband's world. Similarly, these domestic shots of Anna Magdelena are softer diagonals achieved largely because there is no compositional strengthening (by ornate walls or massed groups of people) of the diagonal line in the frame. For example, in the opening minutes of the film we see Anna Magdelena playing the clavichord in front of a wide sunlit window which is square to the camera, while she is at an angle to it.

In another sequence, the film juxtaposes a deep space shot of Bach conducting a large orchestra and choir in a rich baroque setting of intricate architectural curves, overwrought sculptures of Putti. The camera moves back slowly as the music progresses, revealing more rich details. This is followed by a long shot of Anna Magdelena playing in the same room as before with a child playing at her feet enrapt in a game and listening to the music. In this shot the camera moves slowly forward as her voice-over informs us of the music's source. The shot cuts away to a close-up of the published music sheet, her voice carrying over the cut. Thus in three shots Straub and Huillet weave the public, the private, the ornate, the simple, the financial, the godly and the natural. The latter contrasts are assisted by the subtle device of light entering windows. At the far end of the baroque hall, the light luminously and unnaturally floods the high windows like an ethereal spiritual light, while in Anna Magdelena's room it is a natural sunlight. It is as if the film-makers had provided visual renderings of the two sides of Bach's music – the public ceremonial homage to God, and the other a more private intimate expression of ordinary human emotions.

One of the running themes in the film is death, that of many of Bach and his wife's young children. Told in the matter-of-fact voice of Anna Magdelena, nevertheless its emotional expression is provided in the music and the film's framing and editing in which personal grief and sadness pervades. As Bach's death approaches, a more romantic and subjective view is given in the film, as he is shot in chiaroscuro-lit close-ups, complicating any view of the film as purely formalist or Marxist. In fact, its mood is much more Bressonian in its sense of grace.

The profound sadness, the extraordinary moving quality of *Chronicle* is expressed through the film as a whole and not through 'expressive' acting. Refusing what may be called the narrative drive of psychologistic characterisation, *Chronicle* allows Bach's music, the narrative of the 'diary' enunciated in an emotionless voice-over and Straub and Huillet's spatial and rythmic organisation to provide the film's emotional expression. This is much more a Bressonian film than a Brechtian one.

This poetic wholeness and desire to reorganise drama in terms of space and time found in Straub and Huillet's films place it closer to the work of such 'avant-garde' film-makers like Kenneth Anger than to the formalist avant-garde. There is the same broad concern with cinematic space and time (compare *Eaux d'artifice* or even Brakhage's *Scenes from Under Childhood* (1968–70) which can be associated with Andrei Tarkovsky, for example, in his film *Mirror* [1974]).

In summary, the New Wave avant-garde poses crucial questions about the definition of the avant-garde, especially as understood by Peter Wollen in his theory of the 'two avant-gardes'. But as we can also recognise, the two impulses have been there since the 1920s and show no sign of going away so long as form and politics are of interest to visual artists. It is also worth bearing in mind that history is never as neat as the categories used to understand it, and that radical politics can be found in the formalists and innovative form in the political film-makers. What seems more crucial are their reference points – for the formalists it is usually, although not entirely, the fine arts of painting, sculpture and so forth, and for the politicos it is mainstream cinema and the mass audience, but again not exclusively.

1   For example, Barton Byg's book on Huillet and Straub (1995) does not offer a real distinction between these terms.

8   THE 1960s: SEX, DRUGS AND STRUCTURE

The European New Wave had its impact on American cinema too. Interestingly, Lithuanian émigré Jonas Mekas, a key figure in the 1960s underground movement in New York, was a supporter (though a vacillating one) of the work of film-makers such as Godard and Resnais (see Turim 1992). In 1955, Mekas helped found the influential film journal *Film Culture* which attempted to forge a New American Cinema represented by John Cassavetes' *Shadows* (1961). Initially, the journal had a strong European bias. One of its models for an American cinema cut loose from Hollywood, was post-war Italian neo-realism. Its writers included the European exiles Lotte Eisner and Siegfried Kracauer. However, Mekas and the journal began to identify more with an avant-garde impulse as a result of the impact of the growth and burgeoning underground film movement (Pruitt 1992).

New York was to become the avant-garde centre in the 1960s and this chapter discusses three of the filmmakers living and working there during this period. All three were responsible for classic films of the 1960s avant-garde – Jack Smith's *Flaming Creatures* (1963), Michael Snow's *Wavelength* (1967) and Andy Warhol's *Sleep* (1963) (there are others in the case of Warhol – *Empire* [1964] and *The Chelsea Girls* [1966]). Smith's and Warhol's films reached beyond the small but highly influential avant-garde enclave to access a wider audience (Barnes 1993; Wolf 1997). Their notoriety attracted Hollywood directors, European film auteurs and writers. They were all exemplary of film as avant-garde art, and were made in a hot-house art world centred in New York in the 1960s that was similar to the 1920s situation in Europe discussed in Chapter 3. Avant-gardes were being forged across nearly all of the arts, including sculpture, poetry, dance, music, theatre, performance and video in New York. The 'undergound film' explosion was part of this scene.

Warhol was a major Pop Art painter before he turned to film in 1963. He is the only major artist to have taken up film in a serious and sustained fashion, making hundreds of films from 1963 to the early 1970s. His early films represent a watershed in avant-garde cinema. They were largely made in black and white, on a simple camera, using takes as long as the roll of film (100 feet on the Bolex and on the Arriflex) and including the flare-up reel ends. The shot was more often than not perfectly static. These films were also projected at a slow speed of 16 frames per second (since the early 1970s, 18 fps was the norm). They eschewed any editing or effects like super-imposition or camera movement. Their static stillness was accentuated by the slowed-down speed applied paradoxically to fairly unmoving subject-matter – the Empire State Building, portraits where people stared into the camera lens, a man eating a mushroom, couples kissing. It was a deceptively simple aesthetic that included as part of its effect, the duration of film. The spectator experienced the slow passing of time. There were neither narrative concerns, nor formal devices to distract the spectator from the interminable stare of the camera at its object. At one level the film's unity was specified by the length of the film roll, and so most of the early films are structured by such an accident of technology. The nine parts of *Eat* (1964) or parts of *Kiss* (1963) are simply the number of reels, with each reel's flare-up end and beginning replacing the usual neat edit. The seeming banality of this film work is undermined by its compositional and textural beauty and by his choice of those before the camera – painters, curators, models, socialites, poets – many of them natural performers, as was revealed in the sound films he began making in 1965.

While major talents worked through the period and after unscathed by his work – Kenneth Anger, Robert Breer, Stan Brakhage and Harry Smith – his influence on many talents who emerged in the 1960s and after was considerable; they include Michael Snow, Peter Gidal, Malcolm Le Grice,

George Landow, Ernie Gehr, Hollis Frampton, Paul Sharits, Tony Conrad, Joyce Wieland and present-day young British artists like Sam Taylor-Wood, Douglas Gordon, Gillian Wearing and Tracey Emin.

His influence has been two-fold – one in the direction of formal film, as we shall see, and the other in the gritty but ultimately baroque 'realism' of his performance-based work, centred on the 'superstars' he nurtured in the Factory during the 1960s (see Koch 1991). He was influenced in the former by gay porn and in the latter by the Beats and Jack Smith's work.

Narrative and formal complexity, so central to Deren, Anger and Brakhage, was eschewed by Warhol's early silent black and white films which flew in the face of such a tradition by giving the spectator the material thing itself, in this case the images which happen to be captured by film. Like the anti-form sculptures of the late 1960s, the film itself was up for grabs in a profound rock-bottom ontological move by Warhol. These films did not seem to deserve the title of art. They had nothing of the craft of art work. Whatever the feeling about Anger, Deren *et al.* there was usually the recognition of a viable film artwork, albeit one that was thought by some as pretentious, boring etc.

In the case of Warhol's early films there was shocked incredulity that such work could even be considered as art, a reaction that added to his status in the New York avant-garde. This response had much to do with how film had always been understood. While a painting of a mundane object had been perfectly acceptable since the impressionists of the nineteenth century (although it had at the time attracted similar objections), the idea of a film-maker filming an object over a lengthy period of time without any attempt at film construction or story or even drama was anathema. Of course, there is an important difference. To sit through Warhol's *Empire* took hours, whereas one could decide how long to look at a painting. Duration was thus at the core of Warhol's early films.

Sleep

Like many of his early films, *Sleep* is a much maligned and misunderstood work which has rarely been seen in its entirety (see Angell 1994). The myth still circulates that it is a straightforward single take, a fixed shot of a sleeping figure. In fact it comprises quite different shots which at times are heavily edited, repeated sections and freeze frames. The film, made in black and white, is silent and 5 hours 21 minutes long (at 16fps). It was made with the Bolex camera which only took 100-foot rolls, allowing at the most 4-minute takes. According to John Hanhardt, Warhol 'assembled the final movie from a half-dozen repeated, spliced, and looped three-minute reels selected from the rolls he had shot night after night at Giorno's apartment' (quoted in Miller 1994: 14). Unlike *Empire*, made in the same year, it is not an early model of his fixed-frame single long-take films of the next few years and as such its reputation as a conceptual film is misleading. Callie Angell describes it as a 'fragmented, rather abstract, and repetitious assemblage' (1994: 11).

Of iconic, even mythical, status, *Sleep* resists analysis. It also refuses interpretation. It can be argued that it is the film in which Warhol attempted editing, and after which he discovered his long-take aesthetic. We know that he originally planned a much wider array of shooting techniques, including hand-held camera. Particular sections reveal about 100 edits, suggesting an impulse towards the repetitious fragment, rather than the steady flow of the captured reality of the single-take which he aggressively exploited in *Empire* and for some time afterwards, and on which rests his reputation as an important and influential avant-garde film-maker. The film also establishes his interest in people and the genre of portraiture.

John Giorno, the sleeper, is shot with a light source from the right-hand side and in the famous shot of the figure there is a strong shadowy feel to it with deep shadows, especially on the figure's left side of the head where the neck meets the chest revealing the light source to be someway behind the figure. Giorno's chest and shoulder has deep chiaroscuro so that it is difficult to discern where the chest ends and the left arm begins. The light is placed high, just below and to the left of the right nipple. The other strong area of light is the pillow in the upper right-hand part of the frame. This image has full 100-foot reel lengths (over 3 minutes), repeated. The man's head turns from left top right, altering the shadows' shapes and his face's visibility. At times the figure's head turns through a jump cut.

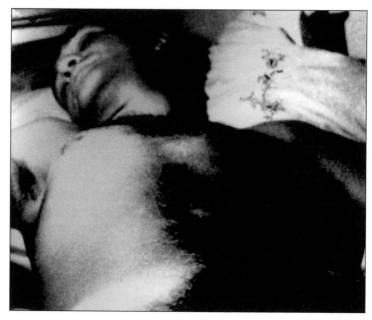

Figure 7 *Sleep* (Andy Warhol, 1963)

Another shot is a profile close-up of the right hand side of Giorno's head, which lies with the chin towards the right side of the frame. The lighting seems more evenly spread but still comes from a source located in the upper left off-frame. It also seems to switch in its brilliance being more muted suddenly, which probably signals an edit or jump cut, but the utter immobility of the sleeping face makes the edit indiscernible except through a change in light tone. The image is 'classical' in style due in part to Giorno's dark, swarthy, Italianate good looks. There is faint movement as the eyeball moves beneath its lid. The reel is defined by the darker light which becomes brighter some time in.

This shot abruptly changes to a more intense close-up during which Giorno moves in his sleep, throwing his arm above his head. The latter part of this movement is repeated before the shot changes to a slightly differently angled one in which the chiaroscuro light falls over much of the shot and the sleeper once again settles himself in a sighing movement. The sleeper's movements are reflected in the slight changes of shot in this section. Of course, in such a film of intense stasis, the slightest movement of shot sets up a quite different patter of light and shadow on the figure. This short segment of slightly different shots is repeated.

Jack Smith

Stephen Koch notes the difference between Andy Warhol and Jack Smith when he contrasts 'the cinematic swirl of rococo flesh in *Flaming Creatures* [1963] with a camera as sinuous and violent as Warhol's was withdrawn and still' (1991: 5). *Flaming Creatures* is a legendary film in the history of avant-garde cinema. Like *Empire* and Anger's *Scorpio Rising*, its reputation goes way beyond avant-garde cinema. Smith has often been lumped together with Anger and Warhol – all gay, camp, outrageous in their time, and all tapping into American popular culture in one form or another. But it is with Warhol that Smith has most affinity, unsurprisingly given the latter's influence on Warhol. Like Warhol, Smith was identified with underground film. For Sheldon Renan 'underground' tends to be identified with the 'artist's unmitigated vision' and small budgets (1967: 51). This view fits Smith perfectly in so far as his work is in a visionary style. *Flaming Creatures* is marked by the strangeness of its images and its uncompromisingly 'shocking' sexual subject matter.

But Smith was also a central figure in New York theatre, with his famous theatre/performance pieces forming part of the New York Theatre of the Ridiculous of which Ronald Tavel, an important Warhol collaborator, was another influential figure. Performance is central to Smith's work. But it is also performance as it is found in certain areas of sexuality – especially the swishy 'drag queen' and transvestite. Associated with this sensibility is a celebration of certain actresses of B-movie Hollywood, the source for drag artists – in Smith's case his life-long obsession with Maria Montez (reincarnated by Mario Montez who 'stars' in *Flaming Creatures*), an echo of Joseph Cornell's with Rose Hobart. Warhol was to exploit this even further with his own use of drag queens like Montez.

Flaming Creatures

In Smith's film mess, chaos, detritus and a Baroque theatricality reigns. For Smith, artifice, revealed yet nurtured, is the whole point of art. There is the sweet smell of decay, of exotic perfumes and less agreeable bodily fluids. And of course there is his often paranoid, non-sequiturs often in

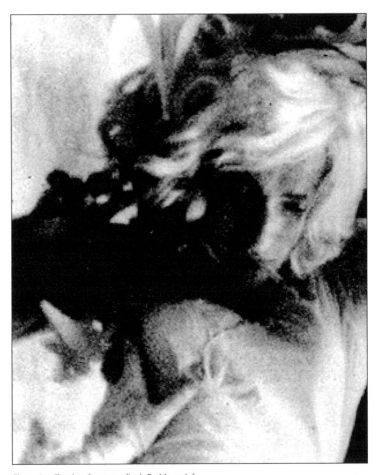

Figure 8   *Flaming Creatures* (Jack Smith, 1963)

the language of fish, Baghdad, fruit, genre-spiel and the invented names by which he achieved symbolic reprisals for the harms and hurts he felt had been inflicted on him by others (often his most stalwart supporters). His cinema has been likened to Erich von Sternberg's 'cluttered shallow space, his veils and mirrors, his chiaroscuro and dramatic overhead lighting, and his sense of theatrical body language and gesture' (Rinder 1997: 143). Jim Hoberman decribes *Flaming Creatures* as

> primitive and sophisticated, hilarious and poignant, spontaneous and studied, frenzied and languid, crude and delicate, avant and nostalgic, gritty and fanciful, fresh and jaded, innocent and jaded, high and low, raw and cooked, underground and camp, black and white and white on white, composed and decomposed, richly perverse and gloriously impoverished. (1997: 155)

Flaming Creatures opens with the mock titles of well-worn print of a low-budget movie, accompanied aptly by the Hollywoodesque oriental music from a Montez film, *Ali Baba and the 40 Thieves* (1944). Shot with very old black and white film stock, it has an antique distressed look, with the whites taking on a shimmering bleached look against the deep chiaroscuro black shadows cast by the dramatic high-spot lighting. Renowned for its polysexual tableaux and orgy scenes, its shock value has been reduced by the intervening years of sexual flagrance in advertising and mainstream cinema. However, its aesthetic and ambience has not been eclipsed by time, and even perhaps enhanced.

It remains one of the most conscious and successful attempts in the avant-garde cinema to engage creatively with the Hollywood dream-machine, its 'cine-glamour'. Juan Suarez has argued that Smith's 'brand of avant-gardism ... favored marginality and disappearance' (1996: 212). For Suarez, avant-gardism, unlike high-art modernism, is to be understood as creatively interacting with low-art popular culture, often caught between celebrating and subverting its base in commodity capitalism. Smith's perennial attacks on landlordism was part of his own slightly exotic socialist stand against an 'avant-garde' which he thought had been colonised by the establishment. Like some surrealists, Smith believed certain products – Hollywood B-movies and their stars – ignored by high art and despised by the Hollywood establishment, encapsulated a spirit of tacky honesty and communication which escaped the glossy commodification of American consumerist culture. It is perhaps forgotten that a film identified with a purely decadent fantasy aesthetic begins with a satire of American make-up adverts. Smith slyly satirises make-up advertising with his own version of the sex-sell fronted by a bearded man in drag!

The film opens with a white textured film-luminosity out of which appears a raven-haired beauty, her hands dramatically clutching either side of her head, a similar-looking woman, her hands in the same position, appears in the foreground blocking out the first woman (almost like a super-imposition), and a man can be seen in the background. On the soundtrack, an Eastern-accented voice whispers: 'Today, Ali Baba comes.' The camera jiggles and moves to a frontal close-up of the first woman, seductively posing, one hand in her hair, for camera, her dark hair merging with the side shadows. The hand-written credits appear. A close-up of legs and torso as white knickers are removed. In these first few moments, Smith's aesthetic of dense figuration, using monochromatic tones, often at the white, light grey end but enhanced by a deep chiaroscuro. In a particular cluster of shot towards the end of the sequence accompanied by Bartok's *Concerto for Solo Violin* transparent white veils waft close-up creating a dream-like atmosphere in which the spectator is drawn into the film perhaps to become lost in its swirling, shifting patterns of light and dark.

The film is a 'document' of Smith and friends at play. It is an immediate forerunner to Warhol's use of the Factory as a place for creative improvisation, the acting out of fantasies. But *Flaming Creatures* is also a highly constructed piece of film-making in which Smith employs various devices to create scenarios that slip continually between dream and a memory of a cinema of innocence, now lost. Part of that loss is expressed in the infantile polysexuality of the infamous orgy scene where bodies mingle in a mood bordering on violence. But the film's overall feel is of Dionysian exultation and anarchy tempered by a nostalgic melancholia.

Joans Mekas was a champion of the film, hailing it along with other films (including *Little Stabs at Happiness* and *Blonde Cobra*) as a new revolutionary Baudelairean cinema which was 'opening up sensibilities and experiences never before recorded in the American arts [creating] a world of flowers of evil, of illuminations, of torn and tortured flesh; a poetry which is at once beautiful and terrible, good and evil, delicate and dirty' (1972: 85).

Flaming Creatures was not the only sexually explicit film of the times. Brakhage had made an explicit film of the birth of his child in *Window Water Baby Moving* (1959). Later, Carolee Schneeman filmed herself and James Tenney making love in *Fuses* (1968). But Smith's use of transvestites, lesbians and other 'queers' in what was a celebratory work attracted the most public and police attention, much to Smith's dismay.

Michael Snow

Unlike Smith, Michael Snow (together with Warhol) was a linking figure between the American and European avant-gardes of the 1960s and 1970s. The success of *Wavelength* was an international one. A series of films made by Snow in the late 1960s and early 1970s (*Standard Time* [1967]; *Back and Forth* [1968–69]; *One Second in Montreal* [1969]; *La Region Centrale* [1971]) served as models of filmic purity for many European avant-garde film-makers. If Snow had learnt about duration from Warhol, he yet forged his own 'complex' style, appealing to the more fine art-based practitioners emerging in Europe. Snow steadily eschewed the more fashionable subject matter of much of Warhol's work for the mundanity found in the 1960s New York minimalist sculpture, with which he was involved. But not immediately, for in *Wavelength*, as we shall see, elements of the Warholian 'performance' persist.

A Canadian based in New York during the 1950s and 1960s, Snow was a prolific experimenter, moving easily between jazz, painting, sculpture, photography, slide-tape and film (see Roberts 2001; *Afterimage* 1982–83). Snow was identified as a leading figure of the structural film movement 'invented' by Sitney in *Visionary Film*. Sitney understood it as moving from 'complex forms' towards a 'cinema of structure' and linked Snow with fellow structuralists George Landow, Hollis Frampton, Paul Sharits, Tony Conrad, Ernie Gehr and Joyce Wieland (Sitney 1979: 369).

We have noted the interchangeability of the terms 'avant-garde' with 'experimental' in relation to film, but no more so than in Snow does the term 'experimental' become most pertinent. His method is often one of taking an idea like a hypothesis and then testing it out in the artifact. Snow is fascinated by the properties of film (and other media) as an illusory representational system: the fast panning of a camera transforming the deep space of the world into the flat texture of *Back and Forth* (1969), the filming of still photographs in *One Second in Montreal* (1969) and the mechanical rotating camera filming the Canadian waste in *La Region Central* (1971). This experimental attitude took a strong grip among film-makers in the years after *Wavelength*, as we shall see in the next chapter.

Wavelength

Snow's classic epitomised the 'structural' film for writers such as Sitney (1979) and Michelson (1971). Even if judged as an impure example of such an aesthetic by Malcolm Le Grice and Peter Gidal in Britain, nevertheless the impression of a single take, the seeming banality of the subject matter and the stress on film form and process, made *Wavelength* a deeply influential film. Interestingly, it is, in fact, a fairly eclectic film – containing conceptual issues (the long-take, zoom shot), philosophical matters (the nature of reality and filmic reality), narrative (the mid-film 'murder') and process (colour filters, edited duration).

As Snow has hinted, the film is closer to a film version of a Vermeer painting in its stillness and emphasis on day-to-day life (men moving furniture to The Beatles' *Strawberry Fields* on a record-player). But it is a film which is constantly transforming itself. It shifts from initially being a documentary of a domestic scenario, to a film-noir narrative fragment, to a formal process-film, to an essay on photographic ontology. But its brilliance lies in these elements, seamlessly and effortlessly, being of a piece. It is this integrity of shape and mood in the film which Sitney recognised.

The structure is a shaping of a form of consciousness, and thus lies within Sitney's understanding of the Romanticist underpinning of the American avant-garde. In other words, the film is a journey from a fairly straightforward realist shot which is then gradually transformed in an impossible way given that it mimics a single zoom. Two levels of time interact, the time of the zoom and thus of the real spectator time and the time effected by image-transformations. A third temporal level can be discerned in the film's final moments as the camera steadily moves into the texture of the photograph of waves with its 'time' of infinity, of perpetual disclosure of materiality itself. Such an implication echoes Kandinsky's fascination decades before with the new scientific insights into the irrationality of so-called basic matter.

The film's fixed camera and single 'viewpoint' unifies its rich forms and content. Though the 'single-take' (actually edited as Le Grice disapprovingly noticed) is reminiscent of Warhol, it is quite different. Snow's working-over of the material, his aesthetic interventions, contrast strongly with Warhol's hands-off method. The common ground for the two film-makers is time. Warhol's slowed-down early films and their subject-matter also suggests a form of temporal experience in which infinity takes its place. For example, the film *Henry Geldzahler* (1964) with its namesake sitting on the couch smoking his cigar, nodding off and enduring the camera's long interminable gaze (100 minutes long) creates a feeling of endless time, the interminable passing away of seconds, a slowing-down of reality and thus time itself. Stephen Koch associates this film style with the intertwined notions of death and narcissism. Likewise Snow's *Wavelength* deals with the time of the movement of the camera across the loft and transforms itself from a realist beginning through a fictional scenario to an abstract zone of colour and the infinite waves of the photograph pinned to the wall. For the viewer, associations of mortality, profound sadness and inexplicable joy are mingled in these final moments of the film.

9   THE 1960s AND 1970s: FORM DEGREE ZERO

As in America during the 1960s, there also was an explosion of avant-garde film activity in Europe, inspired to some degree by the American experience but also developing its own characteristics. While the American 1960s avant-garde grew out of the 1950s underground film and the Beat movement, in Europe there was a more ground-zero approach. There had been isolated European figures, like Austrians Kurt Kren and Peter Kubelka and the German Dieter Rot (see Hein 1979; Weibel 1979), Margaret Tait in Scotland and Jeff Keen in England, who had been working before the 1960s outburst. In fact, Kubelka and Kren were involved in formalist films in the late 1950s, long before the American structuralists.

The European avant-garde was both formally innovative and often polit-ically radical and initially formed a part of 1960s counter-culture (Dwoskin 1975; Curtis 1996; Rees 1999). The autonomy of the artist from the art and state institutions was central to its concerns, at least in its initial phase. It was the period in which the film co-operative movement took hold as an alternative context for film production. The London Film-makers' Co-op (LFMC) was founded in 1966 in response to the new cultural demands of the 1960s and inspired by its Arts Labs precursors and the film co-op set up by Jonas Mekas in New York. However the LFMC was only to become a potent productive force from the late 1960s on (Curtis 1996).

In Europe film-makers often literally experimented with the mechanics of the camera, processor and printer, in a way that was fairly uncommon in American film at the time. At the LFMC film equipment, from camera to printers to processors, was bought cheaply, or literally constructed, allowing film-makers to make a film (black and white) in its entirety from shooting to screening without leaving the building. As importantly, this allowed film-makers to control and physically 'interfere in' the printing and processing process to achieve their own effects (see Gidal 1980). This approach placed film nearer to the manipulations of painting and sculpture, and broke through the technological mystique of film-making, lending it open to a fully-fledged modernism, in the sense of a 'return to the materials'. Modernism was not simply the organisation of certain images, but a laying bare of the image-making process itself, incorporating it or leaving its trace in the resultant film. This marked the 1960s film avant-garde from that of the 1920s (Man Ray was the exception).

By 1970, independent film workshops and screening venues, or organ-ised avant-garde film activity, appeared in Britain, Germany, Holland, Austria, Italy, Switzerland and many other countries (see Dwoskin 1975). At the same time it grasped the importance of internationalism as had its precursor in the 1920s. European international festivals became an important means of communication between film-makers in the 1970s, consolidating the European avant-garde's advances in the 1960s, as did the publication of important books by David Curtis (1970), P. Adams Sitney (1974/79), Steve Dwoskin (1975), Peter Gidal (1976) and Malcolm Le Grice (1977).

Peter Gidal

Gidal had been a youthful visitor to Warhol's Factory (like fellow-American Steve Dwoskin) before moving to England in the late 1960s. This, along with his experience of the films, was to be an abiding influence on his subsequent career. In 1971, he published one of the first books on Warhol. Along with Le Grice, he forged a theoretical framework for the British avant-garde as well as being an activist in the early LFMC. In 1975, he published his infamous tract 'Theory and Definition of Structural/Materialist Film' (Gidal 1996). Many years later, in 1989, he published his book *Materialist*

Film, in which, as the title implies, he shed the 'structuralist' nomenclature which had always been ill-defined in his writings.

From the mid-1970s to the present, Gidal has sustained an aesthetic of colour, texture and camera-movement in order to invoke forms based to some extent on theoretical ideas about representation. To a large extent this filmic stance is a post-war one. There is no real equivalence in the prewar avant-gardes – with the exception of Vertov in certain sequences of *Man With a Movie Camera* and Leger in *Ballet Mecanique*. Having said that, it could be argued that in fact this project has been one of inverse order. The forms he desired were attainable through these particular devices and formal measures. In the most achieved of Gidal's film, this distinction between form and formal elements is not completely sustainable or at least does not satisfy an experiential account of the films in question.

Gidal's own understanding of his artistic project has been attacked for its theoreticism and obscurity. But what is at issue in his work is clear. It is an attempt to push the image, often a purposefully mundane one, to the limit of comprehension without collapsing into abstraction. Thus we are forced to confront its properties. For example, we are made aware of the film's duration, its visual texture and subject matter. Though not part of his conscious project, Gidal's work has a formal restrained beauty more on a par with painting. His meticulous attention to the film image as a total visual experience eschewing any form of narrative. In many ways, Gidal's aesthetic partakes in the modernism of post-war art, especially ideas associated with minimalism and conceptualism.

It is striking that Gidal at times assumes that figuration is to be identified with representation. But as we have seen, representation is also to be found in so-called abstract work, as in the paintings of Pollock, Kandinsky, de Kooning and Mondrian. Much of this work complies with the minimal conditions for representation in a two-dimensional art form, that being a representation of space or depth (Wollheim 1987).[1] Once a flat surface is presented in such a way that it intimates depth or three-dimensionality (usually by a mark made on a surface) then representation, albeit minimal, has been achieved. Now it is a property of film that all things being equal (sufficient light, focus, proper processing and so on), representation is mechanically achieved. Unlike painting, there is no effort beyond this pressing of a button. Surveillance cameras often capture images never seen by anyone. As we have seen this is film's unique quality and at the same time its Achilles' heel with regard to its status as art.

Gidal, like Warhol, has made films on the basis of this simple quality of film. In many ways, Gidal's work is equivalent to the idea of the painter's inescapable production of representation by making any mark on a surface. Of course, the theoretical spin-off, is into the realms of meaning. In semiotic jargon, Gidal denies the idea of an 'empty signifier'.

But what haunts Gidal is that he is not marking the surface but recording an event in the world by means of a representation-making machine – the camera. All things being equal and without denying its properties as a medium, it never fails to represent. Gidal has complicated this issue by filming photographs, hence producing a representation of a representation. Just as a surface is only one for art when it is marked or threatened to be marked by an artist, so the camera pointing at reality cannot fail to represent. But it can fail to be art. For example, the surveillance camera's productions are representations but they are not art. These issues in film aesthetics are central to Gidal's work.

Action at a Distance

Gidal's *Action at a Distance* (1980) was shot in colour, with sound and is about 35 minutes in length. It divides into roughly 3 equal parts. The first comprises the hand-held camera pointing downwards towards the corner of a room – the corner intersection being about one third up from the bottom of the film frame. This section depends on a visual ambiguity of 'what seems to be'. On the left-hand side of the frame is the corner of what seems to be a cloth-covered chair. On the right of the frame is the corner of what seems to be a desk. Both are triangular shapes breaking into the frame from either side. The image wobbles in a rhythmic way like a boat bobbing gently on waves. The second part of the film is an image of an ill-lit room with a barely distinguishable person on a bed covered by an untidy array of blankets and sheets. The camera is shoulder-high looking down on the bed, again for about 15 minutes. The final third of the film is a well-lit shot of a blue book resting on what seems to be an old shiny desk top although it could be simply planks with a patina of scratches. The book is askew and the camera is directly above the objects. The image bobs rhythmically as before. Accompanying the film is a soundtrack of repeated phrases and lines written by Vivian Zarvis, which includes such phrases as 'points of reference' and 'loss and death' and is read in a dead neutral voice by Barbara Daly.

The use of a voice on the soundtrack or any other 'representational' sound is fairly unusual for Gidal. The film has a serene and yet austere quality. One is strongly aware of the film-maker's hand and body behind and holding the camera, looking at the scene now on the screen before us (this assumes, justifiably, that it is Gidal who is actually filming these objects and events). The film is in no sense an abstract film; on the contrary, given its Warholian durational qualities – the 3 sets of objects and events shot for about 12 minutes each – it is intensely representational. Its very point seems to be the representationality of film, evoked here by the long shot, the refusal to light dramatically and *Action at a Distance*'s mundane yet ambiguous 'subject matter'.

The film has an intense personal feel. One of Gidal's most distinctive qualities is his rejection of editing as a function of generating meaning or spectator interest. The steady stare, the austere gaze which projects the image as if to speak, refuses an easy or facile consumption by the viewer. The aggressive overwhelming of the viewer is rejected for the unfolding of the image in an invitation emanating from the film as an autonomous object. The image has an illusory-texture – the grain swims as if it has a depth at the bottom of which is the image, or in which, to put it another way, the image seems to have a literal three-dimensionality through surface texture, through heavy grain and dark subdued colour. Texture surface separates off from the object represented but this does not mean a two-fold experience but a single one in which representationality is depth and space within the screen and the illusion of depth is literally in front of the screen.[2] This 'invitation', this merging with the film-image which is a form of envelopment, is only possible in the durational form of certain avant-garde films, especially with 'materialist' film-makers, such as Nicky Hamlyn, often associated with Gidal. A more aggressive experience is found in films of the same ilk – Kurt Kren's *Baume im Herbst* ('Trees in Autumn') (1960), for example, or Michael Snow's *Back and Forth* (1969), both of which in their in-image movement create aggressive, overwhelming, enveloping optical-based effects.

One of the aspects of Gidal's work is its shunning of the melodramatic, the sensational, the overpowering aspects of a culture, dominated by fragmented projections, traumas and shocks of deep part-object envelopment. On the contrary, in many of Gidal's films a quivering shaking 'reality' is almost tentatively embraced or should we say held at arms length. It is allowed its externality through the stress on the materiality of the film representation. And by materiality it is not meant the purely experimental aspect of avant-garde film in which the camera, projection, screening materials and machines are coaxed to produce their own effects displaced from any respect for the world-as-film-representation.

Gidal's films from the early 1980s onwards excluded the human figure on feminist political grounds. In *Action at as Distance*, however, there is a reclining half-hidden figure in section two of the film. What can we make of this? First, in the other two sections of the film, the first and third, the image is of a space which could only awkwardly contain a figure. In other words, Gidal constructs representational spaces that offer no possibilities for human presence or action. Nevertheless they exude emotion; they seem haunted by absence, like an empty landscape, a melancholic absence.

Malcolm Le Grice

Le Grice and Gidal have always been linked in histories of the British avant-garde. Both prolific writers and propagandists in the early years of the new movement, they were also practically involved in establishing the LFMC and as teachers (see Curtis 1996).[3] Although agreeing over broad concerns, especially the political and ideological role of film, their aesthetics are quite different. Le Grice's work developed rapidly throughout the 1970s and came to an abrupt end with *Finnegans Chin* (1981). With his return to artistic activity in the mid-1980s, he concentrated on the burgeoning computer field and returned to his first love, music, experimenting with computer systems and sound in ways that were reminiscent of the 1920s German avant-garde (especially Eggeling, whom he has cited as an influence).

Le Grice's classic book *Abstract Film and Beyond* (1977) sets out the historical root of what he calls 'formal film'. It is in the history of modernist painting, beginning with Monet and running through Cubism and early abstract art, that Le Grice locates the impulses which will fuel the European avant-garde of both the 1920s and the 1960s. In other words, it is the Greenbergian rejection of realism and naturalism that sustains modernism with which Le Grice identifies as a film artist.

Le Grice's early activities involved both single-screen film and expanded work, which included performance in relation to the screen (e.g. *Horror Film* [1970]). If Gidal's films are austere, at times even severe, in their beauty, stressing texture, grain and compositional forms, Le Grice's delight in colour and movement. He is one of the major colourists of the European formal avant-garde, foregrounding strong primary colours reminiscent of a Pop Art pallette of which Le Grice could be a latter-day member.

Berlin Horse

Berlin Horse (1970) can lay claim to being one of the few classics of the European avant-garde. It comprises two brief films – a race-horse being exercised in a yard; and horses being led from what seem to be burning stables. Le Grice transforms these two short pieces of film (one shot by him in 8mm colour and the other a fragment of an early film newsreel) into a colour-poem of immense lyricism. The two film fragments are submitted to a series of printing operations. Negatives were made of the originals and superimposed on each other, and then further transformed through colour filters.[4] The films are also printed to run backwards. The end result is a complex rhythmic weaving of images assisted by the natural rhythms of the subject matter and brief repetitions of the images. The rich yellows, reds and blues with their solarised effects as if the film is hand-painted, is reminiscent of Len Lye's early colour experiments. On the soundtrack is a bright looped melody by Brian Eno.

There are two-screen and single-screen versions of the film. In its expanded form, the colour-processed film just described is on the right-hand screen while a monochromatic version is on the left. In this way, Le Grice stresses the colour transformations for the viewer and highlights the colour print process that has taken place. This two-screen version has a more formalist feel although its rich sumptious colour and hyperactive subject matter nevers allows this process-visibility to dominate in any way. The more commonly-seen single-screen colour version is highly successful and stands in its own right.

Berlin Horse is an example of the lyrical beauty achieved through a mix of rich sumptuous colour, and internal rhythms achieved through repetitions of brief moments, speeding up, slowing down and reversing the film so that in this case we sometimes see the horse running backwards. The horse is therefore not simply a peg to hang on processes, but in fact emphasises the latter's 'distortion' of 'normal', realist film representation. The same kind of beauty is to be found in the colour-filter sections of Michael Snow's *Wavelength*, which may have influenced Le Grice.

At times in the early 1970s, Le Grice's aesthetic stresses colour. In a film-performance piece like *Horror Film*, he uses the super-imposition of projected colour fields and his own naked body to produce a rich luxuriant array of colours. There is an important tension in his work between conceptual and process-based structures with more painterly ones often reminiscent of the strong colours of 1960s Pop and Op art. But *Berlin Horse* is also a passionate captivating film, whose formalist strategies do nothing to quash its exuberance. In fact they are its form of expression, like a repeated musical phrase around which a melody is spun.

Kurt Kren

Kren is best known for his film 'documentation' of the infamous Vienna Material Action group. He was born in Vienna in 1929 and died there in 1998. He worked in West Germany and the US, and began making films in 1953. Together with Peter Kubelka he is a pivotal figure in the post-war European avant-garde and was a key member of the Viennese Formal film movement of the 1950s (see Weibel 1979). His rigorous hard-edged formalism is peculiarly European, being uninterested in the more Romantic aspirations of the 'visionary' American structuralists as described by Sitney (1979). Kren was concerned with systems and processes long before their centrality in the 1970s. His film *Baum im Herbst* is acknowledged as the first true structural film.

A.L. Rees describes Kren's work as involving 'both chance and order' (1983: 255). For Le Grice, Kren's work embraces process and an existential attitude, by which he means that Kren's work also depicts subjective responses to his experience of the world. For example, Kren's *Baume im Herbst* is a film in which 'the camera as subjective observer is constrained within a systemic or structural procedure' (Le Grice 1977: 101). The film consists of single-frame shots of the branches of a leafless tree with a hand-drawn soundtrack. The result is a rapid aggressive staccato montage with a loud noisy soundtrack. As Le Grice suggests, there is a strong sense of the film being expressive of the film-maker's viewpoint while also being shot according to a system which is not readable from the viewing experience.

15/67 TV

In Kren's *15/67 TV* (1967) he uses subjective-biased shots filmed in black and white through a dockyard cafe window. In the foreground, filling the centre and left of the screen, we see the outline of a man seated at a table. Through a large window on the left side of the screen in the background, we can see a dockside around which three girls are gathered. In another shot with an identical feel we see only one girl sitting on what appears to be a dockside capstan. People pass just in front of the window in the shot's middle ground. The film plays on identity and difference. The five shots are taken from the same point but at different times, each being about two seconds long. The shots are edited together in short clusters divided briefly but noticeably by black frames.

Shots are repeated and there seems to be a system, but it is not dis-

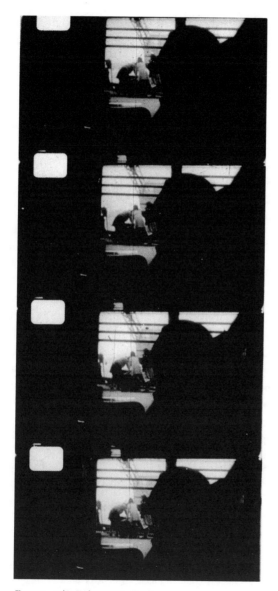

Figure 9   *15/67 TV* (Kurt Kren, 1967)

cernible from a first viewing (or even many more). In fact, it would need a shot-by-shot analysis at the edit bench to reveal fully its structure. Rees remarks that 'the five shots might possibly be segments of a single take' (1983: 255). Kren's documentation for *15/67 TV* shows there is a system even if it is submerged in the film. In this way Kren's aesthetic is not one in which conceptual matters dominate the film except in some general way of forcing the viewer to attend to the film in a way in which an obvious structure would not. Thus his formalism does not overshadow the film, which remains a representational account of a mundane moment in the life of the film-maker.

15/67 TV is an example of an 'abstract' film in the same way as the Man Ray films discussed in Chapter 1 are. 'Reality' as represented through the camera is constructed or abstracted according to principles which highlight formal aspects – in the case of *15/67 TV*, time or duration. A moment captured on film is re-organised through fragmenting (breaking down the shot into shorter shots), editing (re-ordering them) and repetition (time folding back and forward on itself). Unlike Man Ray, the emphasis here is not on abstracting through close-up, solarisation or ambiguity of shot but by organisational processes performed on the film itself, namely editing. In this way, the integrity of the original film is sustained.

The structural film movement dominated as a practice (longer as a theoretical position) until the mid-1970s, after which it suffered a series of blows both from within and without. From within, female film-makers left the co-op to found their own gender-based organisations (Circles and Four Corners). From outside, gay and black film-makers began to draw on other traditions to make their own films.

1 See Wollheim on some cases of abstract art being non-representational, for example Barnet Newman in *Painting as an Art*.
2 The illusion is such that in certain gallery installations, one can approach the screen and seek to 'touch' the swimming texture lying as if just above the screen's surface.
3 See Le Grice's own account of his career in *Filmwaves*, 2001, 14, 15–18.
4 An excellent account of this is given by Le Grice in the documentary *Normal Vision* (Arts Council 1982) based on his work.

10   THE 1980s: THE GHOST IN THE MACHINE

It is against the hegemony of formalist-cum-structural-materialist film of the 1970s that Patrick Keiller, Jayne Parker and Cerith Wyn Evans, who was part of the New Romantic film movement (O'Pray 2001), should be considered. As we have seen, the structural film's aesthetic parameters were governed largely, though in no way entirely, by formal notions such as duration, process and spectator-as-meaning-production. The late 1970s and 1980s marked a fairly radical break with this aesthetic. Rees remarks that 'the pluralism of the late 1970s produced an avant-garde cinema uncertain of its identity and uncomfortably suspended between political, economic, theoretical and aesthetic concerns' (1983: 288). More broadly, it may be argued that there was a shift from asceticism to aestheticism. In an Oedipal reaction, the young film-makers embraced what had been anathema to their elders – subject matter (see O'Pray 2001).

The 1980s in Britain can be seen as a rejection of modernism in its more rationalist formalist forms, and a return to the repressed tradition of modernism – one which embraced the oneiric (Ron Rice, Cocteau), the symbolist (Deren) and the documentary (Vertov, Jennings). It was also a trait that Peter Wollen (1987) identified in the more decorative or ornamental work of the painter Matisse, the fashion designer Paul Poiret and Diagilev's stage designer Leon Bakst. Decadence, with its emphasis on the body, opened up a sexual politics evaded by rationalistic machine-based early modernism. The New Romantics can seen as a later example of this trait.

Among the various strands of the 1980s there was a common return to subject matter outside film's own material and ontological concerns. For example, experimental film-makers like John Smith, William Raban and Patrick Keiller evolved an documentary stance. For Smith and Raban it was primarily located in East London. Smith, like Keiller, approached this documentary project through fictionalised, often numerous, quasi-narratives which played formal concerns against witty subjects, as seen in *Shepherds' Delight* (1980–84). But his East London locations in *Girl Chewing Gum* (1976), *The Black Tower* (1985) and others mark them as remarkable reflections on everyday life. Raban's films – for example *Thames Film* (1986) and *A13* (1994) – were more explicitly social and political in their stance, depicting the cultural transition that enveloped East London under Thatcherism in the 1980s. In a quite different vein, the work of Jayne Parker introduced a symbolist narrative centred on performance, ritual and an almost surrealist sensibility. Importantly, Parker discovered the 'nude' genre for film, winning her few friends in the feminist camp but in fact demonstrating prescience given the upsurge of interest in the body in art by the late 1980s and 1990s.

The short-lived New Romantics movement produced a cinema of what at the time seemed untrammeled excess, not only in its rich colour and the elaborate theatricality of its *mise-en-scène*, mixing the exotic, high-art icons and images taken from suspect areas of culture, but also in its blatant sexual imagery culled from performance art, fashion and gay pornography (O'Pray 2001). It was closely associated with the energetic and infamous London club scene of the time. It was also the first British film-movement to take up and push the gay eroticism of Warhol's film work through a Jarmanesque aesthetic. However, as is the nature of these things, the movement lasted only a few years, roughly from 1979–86, reaching its peak between 1982–84. Its main activists were Cerith Wyn Evans, John Maybury, Holly Warburton, Steve Chivers and Michael Kostiff. Other film-makers and artists were associated with them, including Roberta Graham, Jo Comino, Cordelia Swann, Richard Heslop, Dan Landin and Jill Westwood. Nearly twenty years later it can be seen as the last coherent avant-garde film movement in the tradition which lies outsides art institutions.

Wyn Evans and Maybury held a provocative two-person film show at the ICA in 1981 when Evans had not yet completed his RCA course. They were also included in the film sessions of the New Art show at the Tate Gallery in 1983, and were central figures in the Super 8 phenonenon that emerged in the mid-1980s. Maybury had worked with Derek Jarman on *Jubilee* (1978). Interestingly, their contribution was acknowledged by Kobena Mercer in the context of a discussion of 1980s black cinema which emerged in the wake of the New Romantics, when he remarked that 'the 1980s have seen a reaction against asceticism, demonstrated in the opulent excess of the "new romantics"' (1988: 19).

Part of the reason for this lies in the acknowledgement of more culturally visible 1980s work which was deemed to be experimental – namely, the films of Sankofa, the Black Audio Film Collective, and individuals like Isaac Julien and the feature-film work of Derek Jarman, Peter Greenaway and Sally Potter, who moved from the experimental area into experimental/ art-cinema feature-film production in the 1980s. The energies of the avant-garde were absorbed into a new art cinema in Britain comprising the latter figures, joined in the 1990s by Patrick Keiller (O'Pray 1996).

The New Romantics thus formed a genuine avant-garde movement. It was initially unfunded and eked out a precarious existence in small clubs, galleries and fringe venues. It was politically offensive and for that reason denounced as regressive and decadent. The movement also gave the amateur guage Super 8 its strong presence in the mid-1980s. Cheaper than 16mm, it had a different visual feel, but was difficult to edit (which maybe accounts for the blocking-in sequences in the films). Fast editing would have been extremely difficult. By 1984 Wyn Evans was using fairly up-to-date video editing effects in order to manipulate the image/colour – *Epiphany* (1984) is a good example of this. The New Romantics were aware of the new possibilities of video – and were at the forefront of the cross-over between video and film, although for distribution and exhibition 16mm was used, as in *Epiphany* which was transferred to 16mm. Music was hard to marry onto Super 8 print so music cassettes were employed, allowing different tracks to be used for the same piece of film. The elaborate *mise-en-scènes* with painted backdrops, costume, chiarascuro lighting effects – all highly controlled interiors – meant that exterior shots were a rarity.

Like the original 1960s avant-garde, which led to structural film, the New Romantics were, although fairly apolitical, part of an influential post-punk sub-culture, which included the burgeoning club scene, music (Psychic TV, The Fall), dance (Michael Clark), performance (the Neo-Naturists, Lindsey Kemp, Japanese Sankai Juku theatre, Leigh Bowery), painting (Mannerist, Neoclassical) and fashion. Literature replaced theory – especially Leautremont, Burroughs with Bataille. For its influences and inspiration the film-makers leapfrogged a generation – back to the 1950s and 1960s of Andy Warhol, Jean Cocteau, Kenneth Anger, Jack Smith, Ron Rice, Jean-Luc Godard, Rainer Werner Fassbinder and Japanese cinema.

In its aesthetic it celebrated artifice and images pillaged from both high art and popular culture. It emphasised the body, performance and sexuality, notably gay. In many ways it was a move from a Vertovian conception of film as the politics of perception to an Eisenstinian one (found in his later work) of the *gesamkunstwerk* and the 'synchronisation of the senses' (Eisenstein 1953: 60–91). This meant a shift from the materialist-realism of the Le Gricean formalists, to montage and collaging techniques in which the assembling of images took precedence over the shot of reality. But it is also useful to see similarities in Le Grice's own excess of colour and form in *Berlin Horse*. With its implication of sexual and cultural subversion, the New Romantic movement occupied the 'underground' version of avant-gardism.[1]

Epiphany

Epiphany was originally a 50-minute film comprising video and Super 8 work which was edited together and then transferred to 16mm film. The soundtrack was put together by Cerith Wyn Evans and Genesis P. Orridge of Psychic TV. The New Romantics' films were filled with bodies: the whole point of the camera seemed to be to capture the body. In *Epiphany* the body acts out parts – the gay masochist, the skinhead, the

Holy Communion girl, the masked mannequin-like gay lovers – and at other times the film contains documentary-cum-diarist style of young men posing narcissistically for camera, and by implication for the film-maker as well. At times we see a close-up of a skull. The close-up of performance artist Leigh Bowery's painted, chained face runs throughout – a presiding spirit. There is a certain wit in *Epiphany*'s campness and irony. Towards the end, in the scenes of the threatening skinhead and the young Holy Communion girl, sentimentality and nostalgia of sadness, of loss, breaks through. It is a film more of promise than of actual achievement. It is also a film of experimenting – a young film-maker greedily trying out as many tricks as possible.

The film has no obvious structure but is like a series of fantasies linked together largely through music. As a poetic reverie it perhaps works. If it refuses narrative it equally refuses any formal shape or structure. Images drift in and out, sometimes gaining some kind of autonomy only to drift away or be obscured by other images. Only in the last five minutes does the film settle on image clarity. It is a particular gay litany culled from the tradition that had been repressed in the British avant-garde to that point.

Epiphany is a narcissistic tract in which figurations, actions and style set out to shock, to transgress, but in a languorous Pateresque kind of way. It was a gauntlet thrown down at the political-wing of the gay movement and at the formalist film-makers. Social consciousness is not on the agenda, instead a swooning loss of the self jostles with high-art camp. Donald Kuspit (2000) has argued that advanced guard of modernism has been at the expense of a repressed decadence. In the 1980s these decadent images were shocking to the old Left and formalists. Of course, the irony was that the original Co-op movement was born in the 1960s – an equally ambivalent political period. It was in the late 1960s and early 1970s that the Left came to centre stage.

The film's persistent reference to painting is fascinating and while obviously not new in the history of experimental film, nevertheless takes on a specificity here. Le Grice had already returned to paintings in *After Manet* (1975). In Wyn Evans, the presence of painting is quite different and complex. Le Grice's films are reworkings of modernist perceptual issues, for example the reconstitution of *Déjeuner sur l'herbe* (1863) using four screens, and the stop frame filming to attain the mutiple surface decomposition of Cezanne's work in *Academic Still Life* (1976).

For Wyn Evans painting becomes a radical subject matter, literally in *Epiphany*'s use of particular classical painting as a backdrop, which included Girodet's *The Sleep of Endymion* and works by El Greco. The tortured elongation, decadent form of the figure is Wyn Evans' calling-card, an attempt to give credibility for the film's own sensibility. But it is more than that – in front of a classical painting a young louche male model dressed in classical costume, poses flirtatiously, anachronistically smoking a cigarette as he takes a breather, gazing into the camera, at the film-maker – reconstructing the traditional role of the painter's model.

If *Epiphany* is a celebration of artifice then it is a knowing one – the preening youth breaking his classical pose and the young girl's sigh of boredom is at the heart of the self-reflexive aspect of the film, and it treads an unsteady line between a serious exhibition of artifice and a scepticism as to its authenticity – this is a short step from a cultural and perhaps sexual pessimism, making the film quintessentially Warholian.

In support of the painterly aspect of *Epiphany*, Wyn Evans embraces an aesthetic of frontality and of shallow, often confused, depth, using densely-layered super-impositions and complex image-levels – for example, figures acting out before screens of images of bodies and their parts, onto which another figure is super-imposed. The layering achieved here with some play made on the screen plane is painterly compared with the deep-space realism of formalist/conceptual film-making, in which the camera's ability to achieve the representation of 'natural' perspective, so to speak, is largely taken for granted (Gidal is more the exception).

Patrick Keiller

To varying degrees, Patrick Keiller also shared with Cerith Wyn Evans, Derek Jarman and, as we shall see, Jayne Parker, a deliberate engagement with popular culture, or at least the culture at large. Keiller also took advantage of a film tradition that was not confined to the formalist modernist tradition of Le Grice, Gidal and the Co-op movement of the 1970s. For Keiller, the function of landscape in a broad range of films and television from Renoir to *Z Cars*, was pertinent to his own project of documenting contemporary Britain in a series of short films, which included *Stonebridge Park* (1981), *Norwood* (1983), *The End* (1986), *Valtos* (1987), *Clouds* (1989) and his first feature-length film *London* (1994) (see Keiller 1983).

Keiller was trained as an architect and some of his first pieces were slide-tapes depicting a modern building which combined a kind of modernity with a sense of visual incongruity or 'strangeness'. The precursor of this sensibility is perhaps the famous anonymous surrealist photograph from the surrealist journal *Minotaure*, of a discarded, marooned railway locomotive half-buried in foliage (see Foster 1993: 25–9). It is an example of the uncanny. However, this visual and cultural incongruity is not confined to surrealism; it is also found in the films of Eisenstein and Vertov among others. For example, the emergence of the lumpen-proletariat from the holes in the ground in Eisenstein's *October* has a similar potency, combining a rationalised architectural form with pantomime and the grotesque. This sensibility stems partly from the FEKS movement in the Soviet Union of the time but also chimes with 1920s Surrealism. This avant-garde penchant for sublime juxtaposition, the grotesque and music-hall permeates the 1920s and especially the 1930s, when Surrealism filtered through to countries like Britain – as is witnessed in another more important precursor of and influence on Keiller's work, Humphrey Jennings. In this vein, Keiller evokes what Catherine Lacey (1996) called the 'poetry of fact', placing him firmly in the British documentary tradition.

In Keiller's films, as in the other artists in this chapter, there is a return to the 1930s 'advanced guard', a strong sense of the poetic married to a desire to document the world. But in the case of both Keiller and Wyn Evans there is also a sense of malaise. Both titles are end-games, finalities – the 'epiphany', the intense moment of enlightenment, and literally 'the end' – but of what? Both confrontations with moments, with their air of something complete or completing. No longer is it the process that matters – that is over. Something else, more total, a temporal endpoint (*The End*) or escape (*Epiphany*), is desired.

Keiller's early films are marked by their first-person viewpoint, albeit through a 'fictional' voice-over (Keiller 1983). Films like *Stonebridge Park, The End, Valtos, Clouds,* and even his feature film, *London,* are fiction-alised first-person accounts of the state-of-the-nation (and of Europe in *The End* and *London*). Their form is essayist or diarist. Often philosophical, they are nearly always redolent of a languid, ironic distance. The images sometimes match the words – but usually they depict their own world, one that lies outside the uttered words. Keiller's films have a melancholic air of one who is casting his eye on things slipping into the past; beneath the narrator's reveries, intentions and soliloquies on life the world inexorably flows ('dawn awaits the constructed efforts that everyday confound the pessimist', his narrator utters over a deserted town square in *The End*).

The End

The End is Keiller's most overtly surrealist film and, unlike much of his later work, it crosses the Channel and becomes a European film reminiscent of early English 'travel' writers like Daniel Defoe and Lawrence Sterne (quoted in the text and a surrealist *avant lettre*). To underline this Europeanness, he employs as the protagonist the actor Vladek Sheybal whose distinctive world-weary mid-European cadences establish a mood of political and cultural irony and malaise. It is Keiller's homage to an actor who graced many British films of the 1960s and 1970s. Sheybal succeeds in distancing the film from any conventional English perspective. The plangent music (Brahms) cuts in abruptly at times, as in a Godard film, adding to its European art-movie feel. The voice is one of loss, malaise and stoical for-titude. The camera at times is hand-held, reminiscent of a personal tourist view. Often the reel is allowed to run out. Travelogue, geographical facts, superstition, science, sociological comment, economic facts, philosophy and poetic reverie stud the soundtrack.

In mock-surrealist fashion *The End*'s credits inform us that it is a pro-duction of the 'l'ufficio d'inversion'. Intertitles appear at times announcing 'The Threat' and 'a helmet', part of an irrational structuring device. Urban architecture as an expression of melancholia and rural spaces comprise much of the image-track. At times the framing conjures an alienated world surreal in its emptiness and reminiscent of Antonioni's monochromatic films of the early 1960s. In an early shot in the film, he even depicts a mushroom-shaped tower – surely an homage to Antonioni's tower in the Rome EUR district in the first sequence of *L'eclisse*.

The End is a steady accumulation of shots of landscapes and towns, industrial sites, roads and railways stations. A static shot of a busy, wet-surfaced motorway raked by a low sun is counterpointed by a long shot of what seem to be church towers jutting out of a rural scene in a strange thundery light. But there are also many hand-held shots, often rather shakey pans accentuating the personal nature of the film and perhaps the narrator's hand behind it too. There is a surreal air of urban alienation, rural bizarreness and delapidation and decay.

Jayne Parker

At the time of the emergence of the New Romantics whose screenings she attended, Jayne Parker, was having difficulties in feminist quarters with her use of the naked body – both male and female – in *I Dish* (1982) and her disturbing video *Almost Out* (1984), featuring a physical and psychical confrontation between the film-maker and her mother, both naked. While Parker's style is always pared down, and in the past often in black and white, nevertheless her interest in the body placed her in an awkward situation in relation to the film avant-garde's orthodoxy at the time.

Like Wyn Evans, Parker's films take the human body as their subject-matter. But Parker's 'body' is stark, isolated and confrontational. There is a choreography but in the Deren sense and not like Wyn Evan's theatricality, with its exotic costumes and body paints. For Parker, the body is a way of reminding us of the limits of meaning and at the same time of its expressiveness. By and large, her films are intensely visual and anti-literary, shunning words (*Almost Out* is a counter-example, though strictly speaking a video piece), but working specially with music to the point that much of her recent work seems to take music and its performance as its subject matter (see Rees 2001).

In many of her films Parker plays the 'protagonist' – for example, *K* (1989) and *The Pool* (1991) – thus placing her in Sitney's psychodrama genre. But there are strong differences. Her performances are extremely controlled to the point of a repressiveness; her scenarios are minimal and there seems no urgency to render dreamlike states or metaphors of consciousness. Symbolic narrative is rooted in the real world of washing dishes, municipal baths and rooms. For Parker, the body is no more nor less than a body. We are aware of its materiality, its irrefutable 'thereness' as the inescapable conduit in many ways of what we are. Neither do Parker's films suggest some tragic dualism in which mind and body are forever struggling (the modern version being body and text). On the contrary, the body or at least *her* body, is expressive in some fundamental primitive sense.

The Pool

Dance and posture are both archaic and everyday modes of expression in much of Parker's work. *The Pool* opens with two juxtaposed sequences. In the first, Parker, naked, stands poised to dive at the pool's edge. A series of close-ups of her face, feet and lower torso are intercut with her attempts to stifle a nosebleed with the back of her hand while remaining in her stance. A sense of bodily control and preparedness is established against the uncontrolled bleeding. There is a sense of stoic endurance towards the body's insistent leakage.

The sequence switches to her in a classical dance with a man, both of them dressed in dance-wear. The dance comprises a series of movements in which the man repeatedly catches and holds Parker. Control here is matched by trust and the sense of something rehearsed and understood as she falls or jumps confidently into his arms. Again the camera is medium shot, often just framing their torsos, legs and arms. These two sequences are followed by one depicting a large lugubrious fish swimming underwater, its eyes staring coldly, but its movements strong, purposeful and natural. Many of her films include water creatures – fish and eels (*I Dish*, *RX Recipe* [1980], *Snig* [1982]). In *The Pool*, she holds a large fish/eel in her arms.

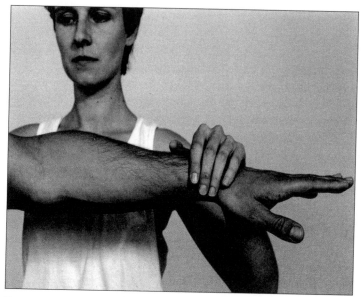

Figure 10   *The Pool* (Jayne Parker, 1991)

The fish can obviously be seen as a phallus-symbol but its associations are richer. Fish/eels also seem to suggest an aspect of inner life – the weight of thought itself, something that is both free and at the same time heavy and dead-like, something that stands as a form of test for her. Although the eel may rather obviously suggest some aspect of maleness – as is suggested in *Snig* when eels are revealed wriggling repulsively beneath the the white bed sheets – they are at the same time cherished. That they come from inside is given more credence in *K* where Parker, again naked, draws animal intestines from her mouth. Long, slimey, grotesquely animal-like, the film echoes the later *The Pool*.

Thus a kind of Freudian mythology meets a more primitive one of oral birth. As in the fish which she holds, and in *Snig* wraps in bandages, Parker proceeds to literally knit the lengths of intestine in a parody of women's 'work' or perhaps of 'mental' working out. There is little doubt that her films, with their ambiguity towards 'taboo' or horror-filled experiences (especially orally-based ones), can be read in terms of Julia Kristeva's (1982) notion of the 'abject'. But they also suggest a fascinating merging and identification of the inner and the outer, of the body and mind. This is not metaphorical, but rather it expresses Freud's own view that the physical, in infancy especially, is a model for the mind.

What is notable about these three film-makers is their disparity of style and attitude. The idea of experimentation or formal exploration is not central to their work at all. There is a strong sense of a subject-matter external to the artist and their art. There is also, if somewhat tentative and ironic, a return to symbolic forms. In other words, they show some faith in the meanings of their images not being simply internally determined but somehow resting on a consensus – one shared with their audience. The body, the landscape, the painted face are drawn from history and culture and hope to resonate with us. This is a fundamental shift from the formal delights and conceptual wit of the structural film movement.

[1] Things are never neat – Le Grice's *Berlin Horse* is very much a film using super-imposition, colour, music and so on, *and* the collage aesthetic.

The films and videos of Sam Taylor-Wood, Gillian Wearing and Douglas Gordon are now firmly entrenched in the mainstream gallery world. Since about 1996, the moving image has come to occupy the very heart of the art world. To take an important statistic – in the British Art Show of 1996, 9 artists out of 25 showed video or film (see Cork 1995). This was a dramatic breakthrough of the new moving-image media into the art world which for decades had shunned it. But in many ways it has put a strain on the British avant-garde film's identity which has been largely established in the 1960s in Europe and America. In fact the young British artists seem to represent a postmodernist tendency rather than an avant-garde one (see Darke 1996). No longer does the idea of 'progress' in the arts seem a valid one, or at least a meaningful one, among young artists. A pluralist approach reigns in which the past is not something to be built upon or developed but rather pillaged and looted.

If we take some of the most successful of these film-making artists – Gillian Wearing, Tacita Dean, Sam Taylor-Wood, Georgina Starr, Douglas Gordon, the Wilson Twins, Steve McQueen – there is little to suggest a coherent direction, or any strong sense of the traditions discussed in this book. Nevertheless, influences exist and connections can be made. Wearing, for example, seems to engage with the television documentary form and with Warholian conceptualism; Dean's experimental landscape infected by diarist-based narrative is reminiscent of Chris Welsby's landscape films of the 1970s; Taylor-Wood meshes Warholian single-take cinema with New Hollywood performance 'excess' *à la* John Cassavettes, Francis Ford Coppola, through Harvey Keitel, also with a growing fascination for earlier classical painting, especially in her photographic work (see O'Pray 1996). Starr is a conceptual-dadaist. Gordon's reworks of mainstream cinema are in a long lineage from Cornell, through Bruce Conner to Ken Jacobs. McQueen, at times, suggests a sensibility close to Maya Deren. What is stark about all of them is the strong incursion of popular culture forms in their work, in contrast to the New Romantics whose interest was in sub-cultures. Most of them had barely any connections with the established British film avant-garde.

This is a very disparate bunch of artists in terms of film and video work. If there is a ghost haunting these works, in some cases causing a distinct din, it is, inevitably, Andy Warhol. Wearing's *Sixty Minute Silence* (1996) for example, is pure Warhol without the latter's monochromatic beauty or superstar frisson. Its subject matter ironically accentuates its refusal of the Warholian 'superstar'. Taylor-Wood has openly acknowledged Warhol's influence, especially in *Killing Time* (1994) and *Methods of Madness* (1994), while Douglas Gordon's slowed-down *24 Hour Psycho* (1993) is Warholian through and through. What perhaps is a common theme in this fairly different work is the prominence of the human figure. Abstraction and studied minimalism are out. Equally they are all borrowers, quoters of past art.

Sam Taylor-Wood

Taylor-Wood's work is distinguished by the potent image of the human figure isolated in the frame. In almost all her major film and video pieces we are confronted by solitary human subjects in various physical and emotional states. They are lethargic, bored, angry, pained; they sing, talk, argue, dance and mime – but they are all united in their fragmented isolation from the world, from each other and from us, the spectator. Whatever the stance or mood, the viewpoint is always singularly objective, establishing an uncomfortable distance achieved by the camera's relentless gaze. At the same time, we are always aware that we are watching a performance, created not for the demands of narrative but for the camera alone. Like Warhol's 'superstars', Taylor-Wood's figures are 'pinned by the camera against a wall of time' (Koch 1985: 87).

Although she draws on iconic images from across the culture, her most sustained engagement is with cinema. On the one hand, she freely pillages images, scenes and the emotional tenor of the films of Coppola, Cassavetes, Abel Ferrara and Martin Scorsese, who have all created a Method-influenced cinema of intense cathartic emotions of extreme, at times excessive, visual power in which the predicament of the human subject is central. On the other hand, she has embraced Warhol's influential early 1960s single-take static-shot films with their pared-down aesthetic and celebration of personality as performance of such 'superstars' as Edie Sedgwick, Ondine and Viva. In fact, the vibrant tension in Taylor-Wood's work is partly the result of this merging of Warhol's minimalist performance-based aesthetic with an ironically delivered full-blown emotionalism plucked from key scenes of the work of Cassavetes, Ferrara and Coppola.

Taylor-Wood's short film *Method in Madness* quite explicitly explores the ambiguities of method acting testing its claims to express some form of authenticity. In the film's ten-minute single-take, a young method actor was asked by Taylor-Wood to 'act out' a mental collapse for camera. Not knowing this, the spectator is uncertain of the nature of what they are watching. Is the young man acting in some straightforward technical sense? Is he playing himself as a form of personal expression? Or is he just simply being himself, whatever that is? There is a profound shift in the film when in the second half of the film, after his histrionic sobbing and crying, he gazes blankly off-shot, depleted and emotionally exposed by his efforts. At this moment, he seems to become himself. His 'performance' of mental breakdown becomes authentic for the first time insofar as he is giving one.

Method in Madness presents a disturbing image and an oddly moving one, of emptiness, vulnerability and utter desolation. Taylor-Wood accentuates the film's bathos by supplying jaunty musak which jangles mindlessly in misplaced accompaniment to this unwitting disclosure of human vulnerability. But is it such a revelation? The question still niggles away as to whether we are unjustifiably reading off these emotional states, from a face of simple exhaustion, or of someone killing time, wondering like Ondine did, 'how much longer do I have to go?'

For Taylor-Wood, the self is always an opaque impossible entity that remains in the shadow of its need to express itself. Voice, gestures, mannerisms, facial expressions are, in the end, inadequate signifiers of self-authenticity. Thus, she is not concerned with the moral dilemmas of film melodrama but rather with the gesture of emotion itself, as an element of representation.

Many of Taylor-Wood's themes are gathered together in *Pent-Up* (1996) – the overwrought emotional states of mind found often in film and music; the invasion of the private by the public and vice versa; the dialectic of the self as full and empty, revelatory and hidden, transparent and opaque, the crisis of authenticity. In many ways it brings her cultural pessimism into true focus, while at the same time offering a redemption, however tenuous, through art at its most reckless, its most manic and its most courageous.

Gillian Wearing

Wearing's documentarist leanings are quite different from the dramatic scenarios of Taylor-Wood. Wearing has experimented with the television interview, separating image from sound in a way which is both humorous and disturbing (see Ferguson *et al.* 1999). She has also 'chosen' subjects for the camera in a more personal, arbitrary way, often treading a fine line between genuine curiousity and bad taste. Of course, Wearing is only tracing the logic of mainstream television's obsession with confessional and exhibitionist modes of entertainment like *The Jerry Springer Show* and *Big Brother*. As A.L. Rees suggests, her work 'reconnects to an underground tradition which elicits the bizarre from the everyday' (1999: 110).

Like Taylor-Wood and others of her generation, Wearing moves easily and continually between film/video and photography. Her work is deceptively simple, often taking the form of interviews which develop ideas posed by that form: who is speaking? Who controls the image? Thus contemporary questions of identity seem central to much of her work. For example, in *2 into 1* (1997), she interviews people about each other and then switches the voices, with people miming others. Fascinating and disturbing at the same time are the two boys and the mother, where the former mouth their mother's remarks about them and vice versa. Beside the odd surreal disjuncture between the age and sex of the person and their voice, one also hears from the mouth of the mother what her sons say about her, as she hears too.

The format owes to the documentary and to the self-revelatory films of Warhol, who used 'personalities' in semi-structured situations and then goaded them off camera to reveal themselves – crossing the line between projecting an on-camera self and something more authentic, less aware momentarily of the camera itself – Warhol's *Beauty No 2* (1965) is a supreme example of this kind of form. Wearing issues improvised enactment in front of camera in her three-screen projection piece *The Unholy Three* (1995–96), in which three disparate but obsessional people are brought together, and what ensues comprises the finished film.

Forerunners of this kind of improvisational, documentary-like cinema (although Wearing largely shoots on video) are the underground performance-based work of Jack Smith, Ron Rice and Warhol. But Wearing seeks her characters in the streets and through adverts. She attracts an off-beatness owing little to the world of avant-garde theatre or street-glamour of Warhol's performers taken from the New York drag culture. Wearing is also more aware of the relationship between the presentation of the self in front of camera and its construction by television through editing and out-and-out manipulation. Her use of characters who wear face masks of famous figures, as in her *Confess all on video. Don't worry, you will be in disguise. Intrigued? Call Gillian* (1994), both allows a freedom to the person under the mask but also, for the spectator, creates odd illusions as we begin to imagine after a while George Bush making the remarks we are hearing (see Ferguson *et al.* 1999). The film is a comment on fame as much as a critique of the culture of the projected personae, the modern-day masque.

In her film loop *Sacha and Mum* (1996) Wearing forsakes the documentary mode for an acted-out 'dance' of domestic love and violence. Though it still has an awkward realist feel to it, using two actors allowed Wearing more control of the choreographing of the struggle between a young girl in her underwear with her old-fashioned dressed mother, which seems to end in an embrace and loving smiles. Are we watching a scene which begins with love and descends into violence or vice versa? It has the air of a scene from a previous decade – 1950s England perhaps – and something of the romance photo-story. Its pacing is unreal – the violence erupts suddenly and equally quickly ends. Projected backwards as well as normally, its repetitive structure and gallery-loop form, together with its distorted grunting whining soundtrack, lend it a bleak, somewhat sordid, feel – it could be an extract from a pornographic film in its home-made and mechanical acting. Its camera angles and editing deny any documentarist reading of the film

In *Sixty Minute Silence* Wearing made her most Warholian piece but with a difference – the one hour-long static shot of policemen and women posed as if for a group photograph is in fact of actors in police uniform. Shown like most of her work as an installation piece (in contrast, Warhol's long single-take films pinned down a seated audience), the audience could treat the installation as primarily a conceptual work, or as making a point about authority, control and so forth. It falls uncomfortably between both renderings and if the audience does not see the final moment when the group relax they also miss a form of dramatic resolutions – the release of tension on the part of the actors, shared by the audience – a moment of bonding between image and spectator – a shared meaningless concentration on the mundane. The video also lacks, purposefully, the monochromatic beauty of Warhol's early films.

Douglas Gordon

Douglas Gordon's work is known for its use of found-film, especially the feature films of Alfred Hitchcock, in his *24 Hour Psycho* (1993) and *Feature Film* (1999), which celebrates Hitchcock's *Vertigo*. He has used instructional films, documentaries and fragments from Hollywood films, as in *10ms-1* (1994), *Hysterical* (1995) and *Confessions of a Justified Sinner* (1995–6). *10ms-1* is a film-loop installation comprising an old grainy medical film of a World War One soldier's hysterical paralysis, a reaction to horrific war conditions. Richard Cork (1995) describes it as a 'gruelling' film but also with an element of 'absurdity' as the man suddenly falls to the ground out of shot, catching the documentary cameraman unawares. The writhing tragic figure who is a victim of a psychopathic illness is an uncomfortable subject matter for the spectator. As in Wearing's *Sacha and Mum*, *10ms-1*'s film-loop form lends a grotesque repetitiveness (like the illness itself one imagines) to the work.

Of course, Bruce Conner had used uncomfortable documentary material in his early found-footage films, memorably of Kennedy's assassination in *Report* (1963–67) and of atomic bomb detonations at Bikini Atoll in the late 1940s in *Crossroads* (1975). But in Conner's case the material is highly worked-over by editing strategies and sound, often using such devices to pose the issue of rendering horror into art. Gordon does not interfere with his material, offering it as some kind of found-object in the surrealist tradition – a convulsive beauty (literally in the case of *10ms-1*).

Figure 11   *24 Hour Psycho* (Douglas Gordon, 1993)

125

This found-object aspect of Gordon's work reaches its zenith in *24 Hour Psycho*'s use of Hitchock's classic iconic film *Psycho* (1960) as a film installation, but in this case interfered with in terms of projection speed, slowing the film down so that it takes a full day to project. This installation has a monolithic quality, both in its time-span (only matched by Warhol's *Four Star* (1966–67)) and in its use of such a classic film. *24 Hour Psycho* is also monolithic in its huge, barely shifting images from a narrative with classic mainstream fast-pacing. Each frame is given a photographic quality which in some sequences renders its subject matter momentarily incomprehensible. Unlike Warhol's film-projection, Gordon's video projection does not have the strong sculptural qualities, the three-dimensionality, provided by the strong, more physical light beam and vulnerability of the projected image (glitches, surface texture, and so on).

The avant-gardeness of these recent artists is questionable, although being taken into the holy sanctuary of the gallery system was the fate of many of the early avant-garde artists. Historical contributions of an avant-garde often herald acceptance into the canon and the institutions and discourses of the art establishment. Many of the younger British artists began their careers in smaller marginal shows before their commercial success. And the work of Gordon, for example, does invite the reaction of 'where is the art in reshowing old movies?' This raises the issue of whether all that shocks in art is avant-garde by nature. A further question may be *who* is shocked – the public (perhaps too easily so) or the art establishment itself (less easily and more of a yardstick)? More interestingly, the traditional avant-garde, so to speak, once based around the Film Co-operative in London, have associated their outsiderness (which is a different matter) with a strong anti-commercial instinct and a desire for autonomy, although this is often compromised by various kinds of government-based funding. Much is murky here as this book stated at the very beginning.

An important aspect of moving-image work of the young British artists is its coincidence with the advancement of video projection technology in the 1990s. In the past, using film projectors in galleries often meant constant breakdowns (overheated motors, snapped films, complicated setups for loops). It was also expensive (it needed a full-time technician on hand at all times to deal with the aforementioned problems). On the other hand, video monitors were too small and projection was of poor quality. This changed with the new digital-based technology leading to sharp imagery and good colour production. Films and videos could be transferred onto highly portable DVDs that meant that extensive exhibitions (lasting weeks and sometimes months) were possible without wear-and-tear and any reduction in quality. The new video projectors produced images that were of a quality that satisfied artists and audiences. This meant that the aesthetic – in terms of scale and projection conditions – was closer to that of cinema even if much of the work was shot on video. However some artists, like Tacita Dean, did stick to the film medium in the gallery using film projectors and complicated but effective film-loop machines. The real impact of this technology is yet to be truly understood but it has meant an ambiguity between film and video. It has also diluted the 'pure' modernist film tradition that stressed film's properties and placed 'video art' in something of a limbo.

Conclusion

It is a paradox of the avant-garde film, set against tradition, that it forms a tradition of its own, one stretching back nearly a century. It is one of the implicit aspects of this book that the avant-garde has been marked by historical 'moments' of intense and often radical activity – the 1920s and 1960s in Europe, the 1960s in New York, the early 1980s in Britain and so on. But these 'moments' have been historically connected by individuals, organisations and discourses that have sustained aspects of those 'moments' and through their own practices often developed them. In most cases these individuals and their organisations have led a precarious existence at the margins of the film and art worlds. The avant-garde tradition is therefore an unusual one in so far as it has never had the security associated with the establishment. Its very fragility, its marginality, has made it more susceptible to enormous change and radical shake-ups. Its weakness is its strength. It could be argued that the proliferation of labels

– avant-garde, poetic, independent film, underground, experimental – is a symptom of this fluidity.

But it may be objected that I have included much more stable and essentially conservative 'moments' in this tradition, for example, that of the European New Waves. This raises the issue of the relativity of the notion of 'avant-garde'. This is especially relevant in terms of the perspective of film-makers. If Brakhage saw himself outside the Hollywood system and to some extent, indifferent to it, Godard saw his work as being in opposition to Hollywood, as a negation of it, hence he was intensely interested in it.

But it also worth standing back from what can become a purely historical and institutional view of these films. What is central to them and more difficult to pin down is what they mean to the viewer. There is little doubt that Godard and Straub and Huillet were perceived as avant-garde at the time. They represented alternative modes of form, themes and experience as much as did Warhol or Snow. To collapse the idea of an avant-garde into simply their means of production and not to take into account their actual impact on viewers would seem to be a rather empty form of understanding film. Hopefully, this book helps in keeping open the idea of avant-garde film as film that seeks to break down barriers, to explode what comes to be taken for granted, even in the avant-garde. Its own refusal to be tied by convention and consensus is also a challenge to the academic, the historian and the critic to do the same.

BIBLIOGRAPHY

The bibliography lists works cited in the text and is also designed to point to useful further reading. The list of 'essential reading' highlights works considered to be of particular importance in the study of avant-garde film, although many valuable contributions are also to be found under 'secondary reading'.

Essential reading

Afterimage (1982–83) Special Issue: *Sighting Snow*. No 11, Winter (includes essays by N. Hamlyn, B. Elder, M. O'Pray and J. Rosenbaum).

Christie, I. (1998) 'The avant-gardes and European cinema before 1930', in J. Hill & P. Church Gibson (eds) *The Oxford Guide to Film Studies*. London: Oxford University Press, 449–54.

Curtis, D. (1971) *Experimental Cinema*. London: Studio Vista.

_____ (1979) *Film as Film: formal experiment in film 1910–1975*. London: Hayward Gallery.

Donald, J., A. Friedberg & L. Marcus (eds) (1998) *Close Up 1927–1933: Cinema and Modernism*. London: Cassell.

Dwoskin, S. (1975) *Film Is ... The International Free Cinema*. London: Peter Owen.

Gidal, P. (1977) *Structural Film Anthology*. London: British Film Institute.

_____ (1989) *Materialist Film*. London: Routledge.

Horak, J. C. (1995) *Lovers of Cinema: The First American Film Avant-Garde 1919–1945*. London: University of Wisconsin.

James, D. E. (1989) *Allegories of Cinema: American Film in the 1960s*. Princeton: Princeton University Press.

Kuenzli, R. E. (1987) *Dada and Surrealist Film*. New York: Willis Cocker & Owens.

Le Grice, M. (1976) *Abstract Film and Beyond*. London: Studio Vista.

_____ (2001) *Experimental Cinema in the Digital Age*. London: British Film Institute.

MacDonald, S. (1993) *Avant-Garde Film*. Cambridge: University of Cambridge Press.

Macpherson, D. (1980) *Traditions of Independence: British Cinema in the Thirties*. London: British Film Institute.

Manvell, R. (1949) *Experiment in the Film*. London: Grey Walls Press.

Mekas, J. (1972) *Movie Journal: The Rise of the New American Cinema 1959–1971*. New York: Collier Books.

O'Pray, M. (1996) *The British Avant-Garde Film 1926–1995: An Anthology of Writings*. Luton: University of Luton/Arts Council of England.

Peterson, J. (1994) *Dreams of Chaos, Visions of Order: Understanding the American Avant-garde Cinema*. Wayne State University Press.

Rees, A.L. (1999) *A History of Experimental Film and Video*. London: British Film Institute.

Renan, S. (1967) *The Underground Film: An Introducion to Its Development in America*. London: Studio Vista.

Sitney, P. Adams (1979) *Visionary Film: The American Avant-Garde 1943–1978*. London: Oxford University Press.

_____ (1987) *The Avant-Garde Film: A Reader of Theory and Criticism*. New York: Anthology Film Archives.

Smith, M. (1998) 'Modernism and the avant-gardes', in J. Hill & P. Church Gibson (eds) *The Oxford Guide* to Film Studies. London: Oxford University Press, 395–412.

Tyler, P. (1974) Underground Film: A Critical Inquiry. Harmondsworth: Penguin Books.

Wees, W. C. (1992) Light Moving in Time: Studies in the Visual Aesthetics of Avant-garde Film. Berkeley: University of California Press.

Williams, R. (1989) 'The Politics of the Avant-Garde', in The Politics of Modernism. Verso: London.

Secondary reading

Abel, R. (1988) French Film Theory and Criticism 1907–1929, vol. 1. Princeton: Princeton University Press.

Aitken, I. (2000) Alberto Cavalcanti: Realism, Surrealism and National Cinemas. Trowbridge: Flicks Books.

____ (2001) European Film Theory and Cinema: A Critical Introduction. Edinburgh: University of Edinburgh Press.

Angell, C. (1994) The Films of Andy Warhol Part II. New York: Whitney Museum of American Art.

Anger, K. (1989) 'Modesty and the Art of Film', in J. Pilling & M. O'Pray (eds) Into the Pleasure Dome: The Films of Kenneth Anger. London: British Film Institute, 18–21.

Barber, G. (1990) 'Scratch and After: Edit Suite Technology and the Determination of Style in Video Art', in Philip Hayward (ed.) Culture, Technology and Creativity in the Late Twentieth Century. John Libbey/Arts Council of England, 111–24.

Barnes, S. (1993) Greenwich Village 1963: Avant-Garde Performance and the Effervescent Body. London: Duke University Press.

Baxendale, J. & C. Pawling (1995) Narrating the Thirties. London: Macmillan.

Bellour, R. & M. Lea Bandy (1992) Jean-Luc Godard Son + Image 1974-91. New York: Museum of Modern Art.

Bloch, E. G. Lukacs, B. Brecht, W. Benjamin, T. Adorno (1977) Aesthetics and Politics. London: NLB.

Bond, R. (1979) 'Cinema in the Thirties: Documentary Film and the Labour Movement', in J. Clark, M. Heinemann, D. Margolis & C. Snee (eds) Culture and Crisis in the Thirties. London: Lawrence & Wishart.

Bordwell, D. (1993) The Cinema of Eisenstein. London: Harvard University Press.

Bouhours, J-M. & R. Horrocks (eds) (2000) Len Lye. Paris: Centre Pompidou.

Brakhage, S. (1977) Film Biographies. Berkeley: Turtle Island.

Brunette, P. (1998) The Films of Michelangelo Antonioni. Cambridge: Cambridge University Press.

Buñuel, L. (1984) My Last Breath. London: Cape.

Burger, P. (1984) Theory of the Avant-Garde. Minneapolis: University of Minnesota Press.

Butler, C. (1994) Early Modernism: Literature, Music and Painting in Europe 1900–1916. Oxford: Clarendon Press.

Byg, B. (1995) Landscapes of Resistance: The German Films of Daniele Huillet and Jean-Marie Straub. London: University of California Press.

Callie, A. (1994) The Films of Andy Warhol Pt II. New York: Whitney Museum of American Art.

Cavell, S. (1979) The World Viewed, Revised Edition. London: Harvard University Press.

Compton, M. (ed.) (1980) Towards a New Art: Essays on the Background to Abstract Art 1910–20, London: Tate Gallery.

Cook, P (1988) 'Chambers and Corridors: Maya Deren', MFB, 55, 654, 220.

Cork, R. (1995) 'Injury Time', in The British Art Show 4. London: South Bank Centre, 12–32.

Corra, B. (1973) 'Abstract Cinema – Chromatic Music', in U. Apollonia (ed.) Futurist Manifestos. London: Thames and Hudson, 66–70.

Curtis, D. (1996) 'English Avant-Garde Film: An Early Chronology', in M. O'Pray (ed.) The British Avant-Garde Film 1926–1995: An Anthology of Writings. Luton: University of Luton/Arts Council of England, 101–19.

Danino, N. & M. Mazière (eds) (2003) The Undercut Reader: Critical Writings on Artists' Film and Video. London: Wallflower Press.

Darke, C. (1996) 'Avant-Garde Cinema in Europe', in J. Caughie & K. Rockett (eds) The Companion to British and Irish Cinema. London: British Film Institute: Cassell, 167–9.

____ (2000) Light Readings: Film Criticism and Screen Arts. London: Wallflower Press.

de Haas, P. (1984) 'Cinema: The Manipulation of Materials' in DADA–Constructivism: The Janus Face of the Twenties, Catalogue. London: Annely Juda Fine Art, 53–71.

Deren, M. (2001) 'An Anagram of Ideas on Art, Form and Film', in B. Nichols (ed.) Maya Deren and the

American Avant-Garde. London: University of California Press, 267–322.

Drummond, P. (1977) 'Textual Space in *Un Chien Andalou*', *Screen*, 18, 3, 55–119.

Dulac, G. (1988) 'The Expressive Techniques of the Cinema', in R. Abel (ed.) *French Film Theory and Criticism 1907–1929*, vol. 1. Princeton: Princeton University Press.

Dusinberre, D. (1979) 'The Other Avant-gardes', in D. Curtis (ed.) *Film as Film*. London: Hayward Gallery, 53–8.

_____ (1980) 'The Avant-Garde Attitude in the Thirties', in D. Macpherson (ed.) *Traditions of Independence: British Cinema in the Thirties*. London: British Film Institute, 34–50.

Eisenstein, S. (1949) *Film Form*. London: Harcourt Brace Jovanovich.

Elsaesser, T. (1987) 'Dada Cinema' in R. E. Kuenzli (ed.) *Dada and Surrealist Film*. New York: Willis Locker & Owens, 13–27.

Epstein, J. (1978) 'For a New Avant-Garde', in P. Adams Sitney (ed.) *The Avant-Garde Film: A Reader of Theory and Criticism*: New York: Anthology Film Archive, 26–30.

Farber, M. (1971) *Negative Space*. New York: Praeger.

Field, S. (1983) 'Underground 2: Re-viewing the Avant-Garde' *Monthly Film Bulletin*, 50, 596, 234–6.

Fer, B., D. Batchelor & P. Wood (1993) *Realism, Rationalism, Surrealism: Art Between the Wars*. London: Yale University Press.

Ferguson, R., D. De Salvo & J. Slyce (1999) *Gillian Wearing*. London: Phaidon.

Fischer, L. (1976) '1943–1948', in *A History of the American Avant-Garde Film*. American Federation of Arts catalogue, New York, 69–83.

Foster, H. (1993) *Compulsive Beauty*. London: MIT Press.

Gidal, P. (1980) 'Technology and Ideology in/through/and Avant-Garde Film: An Instance', in T. de Lauretis & S. Heath (eds) *The Cinematic Apparatus*. London: Macmillan, 151–65.

_____ (1996) 'Theory and Definition of Structural/Materialist Film', in M. O'Pray *The British Avant-Garde Film 1926–1995: An Anthology of Writings*. Luton: University of Luton/Arts Council of England, 145–70.

Gillespie, D. (2000) *Early Soviet Cinema: Innovation, Ideology and Propoganda*. London: Wallflower Press.

Greenberg, C. (1992) 'Avant-Garde and Kitsch', in C. Harrison & P. Wood (eds) *Art in Theory 1900–1990: An Anthology of Changing Ideas*. Oxford: Blackwell, 529–41.

Grierson, J. (1946) (edited by Forsyth Hardy) *Grierson on Documentary*, London: Collins.

_____ (1998) 'Preface to Paul Rotha's *Documentary Film* (1952)' in I. Aitken (ed.) *The Documentary Film Movement: an Anthology*. Edinburgh: Edinburgh University Press, 115–23.

Hames, P. (1995) 'The film experiment' in P. Hames (ed.) *Dark Alchemy: The Films of Jan Svankmajer*. Trowbridge: Flicks Books, 7–47.

Hamlyn, N. (1982-3) 'Seeing Is Believing: *Wavelength* Reconsidered', *Afterimage*, no. 11, 22–30.

Hammond, P. (ed.) (1991) *The Shadow and Its Shadow: Surrealist Writings on the Cinema*, 2nd edn. Edinburgh: Polyglon.

Hanhardt, J. (1976) 'The Medium Viewed: The American Avant-Garde Film' in *A History of the American Avant-Garde Cinema*. New York: American Film Association, 19–47.

Harrison, C. (1981) *English Art and Modernism 1900-1939*. London: Allen Lane.

_____ (1993) 'Abstraction' in C. Harrison, F. Frascina & G. Perry (eds) *Primitivism, Cubism, Abstraction: the Early Twentieth Century*. London: Yale University Press, 185–264.

Hein, B. (1979) 'The Structural Film', in D. Curtis (ed.) *Film as Film: formal experiment in film 1910–1975*. London: Hayward Gallery, 93–105.

Hess, T. B. & J. Ashbury (1967) *Avant-Garde Art*. New York: Collier Books.

Hoberman, J. (1997) 'The Big Heat: Making and Unmaking *Flaming Creatures*' in E. Leffingwell, C. Kismaric, M. Heiferman (eds) *Jack Smith: Flaming Creatures: His Amazing Life and Times*. London: Serpent's Tail 152-167.

_____ (2001) *On Jack Smith's Flaming Creatures and Other Secret Flix of Cinemaroc*, Granary Books, New York.

Hobsbawm, E. (1998) *Behind the Times: The Decline and Fall of the Twentieth Century Avant-Gardes*, Thames and Hudson.

Hogenkamp, B. (1986) *Deadly Parallels: Film and the Left in Britain 1929-39*. London: Lawrence & Wishart.

Holl, U. (2001) 'Moving the Dancers' Souls', in B. Nichols (ed.) *Maya Deren and the American Avant-Garde*. London: University of California Press, 151–77.

Huyssen, A. (1986) *After the Great Divide: Modernism, Mass culture and Postmodernism*. London:

Macmillan.

Hynes, S. (1976) *The Auden Generation: Literature and Politics in England in the 1930s.* London: Bodley Head.

Keiller, P. (1983) 'Atmosphere, Palimpsest and Other Interpretations of Landscape', *Undercut,* 7/8 125–9.

Keller, M. (1986) *The Untutored Eye: Childhood in the Films of Cocteau, Cornell, and Brakhage.* London: Fairleigh Dickenson Press.

Klein, R. (1993) *Seven Minutes: The Life and Death of the American Animated Cartoon.* London: Verso.

Koch, S. (1991) *Stargazer: Andy Warhol's World and His Films,* revised edn. New York: Marion Boyars.

Koestenbaum, Wayne, (2001) *Andy Warhol.* London: Weidenfeld & Nicolson.

Kovács, S. (1980) *From Enchantment to Rage: The Story of Surrealist Cinema.* London: Fairleigh Dickinson University Press.

Kristeva, J. (1982) *Power of Horror: An Essay in Abjection.* New York: Columbia University Press.

Kuspit, D. (2000) *The Dialectic of Decadence: Between Advance and Decline in Art.* New York: Allworth Press.

Lacey, C. (1996) 'The Poetry of Fact', in M. O'Pray (ed.) *The British Avant-Garde Film 1926–1995: An Anthology of Writings.* Luton: University of Luton/Arts Council of England, 275–83.

Landis, B. (1996) *Anger: The Unauthorized Biography of Kenneth Anger.* New York: HarperCollins.

Lawdor, S. *The Cubist Cinema.* New York: New York University Press.

Leyda, J. (1973) *Kino: A History of the Russian and Soviet Film* (2nd edn.). London: George Allen and Unwin.

Low, R. (1997) *The History of British Film 1918–1929,* vol 4. London: Routledge.

MacCabe, C. (1980) *Godard: Images, Sounds, Politics* London; Macmillan.

MacDonald, S. (1988) *A Critical Cinema: Interviews with Independent Filmmakers.* London: University of California Press.

____ (1993) *Avant-Garde Film.* Cambridge: Cambridge University Press.

____ (2002) *Cinema 16: Documents Toward a History of the Film Society*: Philadelphia: Temple University Press.

Macpherson, K. (1998) 'Letter to Gertrude Stein', in J. Donald, A. Friedberg & L. Marcus (eds) *Close Up 1927–1933: Cinema and Modernism.* London: Cassell, 14.

Mekas, J. (1972) *Movie Journal: The Rise of the American Cinema 1959-1971.* New York: Collier Books.

Mendik, X. & S. J. Schneider (eds) (2002) *Underground U.S.A.: Filmmaking Beyond the Hollywood Canon.* London: Wallflower Press.

Mercer, K. (1988) 'Sexual Identities: Questions of Difference', Special Issue, *Undercut,* 17.

Michelson, A. (1966) 'The Radical Inspiration', in P. Adams Sitney (ed.) *Film Culture.* London: Secker & Warburg, 404–21.

____ (1976) 'Toward Snow' in P. Gidal (ed.) *Structural Film Anthology.* London: British Film Institute 38–44.

____ (1984) *Kino-Eye: The Writings of Dziga Vertov.* University of California Press.

Miller, D. (1994) *Billy Name: Stills from the Warhol Films.* New York: Prestel.

Monaco, J. (1976) *The New Wave: Truffaut, Godard, Chabrol, Rohmer, Rivette.* New York: Oxford University Press.

Montagu, I. (1980) 'The Film Society', in D. Macpherson (ed.) *Traditions of Independence: British Cinema in the Thirties.* London: British Film Institute.

Moritz, W. (1997) 'Restoring the aesthetics of early abstract films', in J. Pilling (ed.) *A Reader in Animation Studies.* London: John Libbey, 221–7.

Mulvey, L. (1989) 'Visual Pleasure and Narrative Cinema', in L. Mulvey *Visual and Other Pleasures.* London: Macmillan, 14–26.

____ (1996) 'Film Feminism and the Avant-Garde', in M. O'Pray (ed.) *The British Avant-Garde Film 1926– 1995: An Anthology of Writings.* Luton: University of Luton/Arts Council of England, 199–216.

Nochlin, L. (1967) 'The Invention of the Avant-Garde: France, 1830–1880', in T. B. Hess & J. Ashbery (eds) *Avant-Garde Art.* New York: Collier Books, 1–24.

Nowell-Smith, G. (1997) *L'avventura.* London: British Film Institute.

O'Pray, M. (1996) 'The British Avant-Garde and Art Cinema from the 1970s to the 1990s', in A. Higson *Disssolving Views: Key Issues in British Cinema.* London: Cassell, 178–90.

____ (2001) '"New Romanticism" and the British Avant-Garde Film in the Early 80s', in R. Murphy *The British Cinema Book* (2nd ed). London: British Film Institute, 256–62.

Perez, G. (1998) *The Material Ghost: Films and their Medium.* London: Johns Hopkins University Press.

Petric, V. (1987) *Constructivism in Film: The Man with a Movie Camera: A Cinematic Analysis*. Cambridge: Cambridge University Press.

Pilling, J. & M. O'Pray (1989) (eds) *Into the Pleasure Dome: The Films of Kenneth Anger*. London: British Film Institute.

Pruitt, J. (1992) 'Jonas Mekas: A European Critic in America', in D. James (ed.) *To Free the Cinema: Jonas Mekas and the New York Underground*. Princeton: Princeton University Press, 193–212.

Rees, A.L. (1983a) 'Kurt Kren ... in addition', *Monthly Film Bulletin*, 50, 596, 255.

_____ (1983b) 'Underground 3: Re-viewing the Avant-Garde', *Monthly Film Bulletin*, vol. 50, no. 597, 255.

_____ (1993–94) 'The Themersons and Polish Avant-Garde: Warsaw-Paris-London', *PIX*, no. 1, Winter, 86–101.

_____ (2000) 'The Artist as Filmmaker: Films by Jayne Parker 1979–2000', in *Jayne Parker Filmworks 79–00*. Exeter: Spacex Gallery, 9–30.

Rinder, L. (1997) 'Anywhere Out of the World: The Photography of Jack Smith', in E. Leffingwell, E. C. Kismaric & M. Heiferman (eds) *Jack Smith: Flaming Creatures – His Amazing Life and Times*. London: Serpent's Tail, 139–51.

Roberts, C. & L. Steeds (eds) (2001) *Michael Snow Almost Cover to Cover*. London/Bristol: Black Dog Publishing/Arnolfini.

Rohdie, S. (1990) *Antonioni*. London: BFI.

Rosen, C. & H. Zerner (1984) *Romanticism and Realism: The Mythology of Nineteenth Century Art*. London: Faber & Faber.

Rotha, P. (1973) *Documentary Diary*. London: Secker and Warburg.

Roud, R. (1972) *Jean-Marie Straub*. New York: Viking Press.

Samson, J. (1986) 'The Film Society, 1925–1939', in C. Barr (ed.) *All Our Yesterdays: 90 Years of British Cinema*. London: British Film Institute, 306–13.

Sitney, P. Adams (ed.) (1974) *The Essential Cinema*. New York: Anthology Film Archives/New York University Press.

_____ (1995) *Vital Crises in Italian Cinema*. Austin: University of Texas Press.

Suarez, J. (1996) *Bike Boys, Drag Queens and Superstars: Avant-Garde, Mass Culture, and Gay Identities in the 1960s Underground Cinema*. Bloomington: Indiana University Press.

Tate Gallery (1980) *Towards a New Art: Essays on the Background to Abstract Art 1910–20*. London.

Taylor, R. & I. Christie (eds) (1991) *Inside the Film Factory: New Approaches to Russian and Soviet Cinema*. London: Routledge.

Taylor, R. & I. Christie (eds) (1993) *Eisenstein Rediscovered*. London: Routledge.

Tisdall, C. & A. Bozzolla (1977) *Futurism*. London: Thames and Hudson.

Turim, M. (1992) 'Reminisceneces, Subjectivities, and Truths', in D. James (ed.) *To Free the Cinema: Jonas Mekas and the New York Underground*. Princeton: Princeton University Press, 193–212.

Vergo, P. (1980) 'Music and Abstract Painting: Kandinsky, Goethe and Schoenberg', in *Towards a New Art: Essays on the Background to Abstract Art 1910–1920*. London: Tate Gallery, 41–63.

Weibel, P. (1979) 'The Viennese Formal Film' in D. Curtis (ed.) *Film as Film: formal experiment in film 1910–1975*. London: Hayward Gallery, 107–12.

Wells, P. (2002) *Animation: Genre and Authorship*. London: Wallflower Press.

Willemen, P. (1994) 'An Avant-garde for the 1990s', in P. Willemen (ed.) *Looks and Frictions: Essays in Cultural Studies and Film Theory*. London: British Film Institute, 141–61.

Williams, L. (1981) *Figures of Desire: A Theory and Analysis of Surrealist Film*. Berkeley: University of California Press.

Williams, R. (1989) *The Politics of Modernism*. London: Verso.

Wolf, R. (1997) *Andy Warhol, Poetry, and Gossip in the 1960s*. London: University of Chicago Press.

Wollen, P. (1982) 'Godard and Counter cinema' in *Readings and Writings: Semiotic Counter-Strategies*. London: Verso, 79–91.

_____ (1982a) 'The Two Avant-Gardes' in *Readings and Writings: Semiotic Counter-Strategies*. London: Verso, 92–104.

_____ (1982b) "Ontology' and 'Materialism' in Film' in *Readings and Writings: Semiotic Counter-Strategies*. London. Verso, 189–207.

_____ (1987) 'Fashion/orientalism/the body', *New Formations*, 1, 5–33.

Wollheim, R. (1987) *Painting as an Art*. London: Thames and Hudson.

Wright, B. (1974) *The Long View*. London: Secker & Warburg.

INDEX